P9-BIK-298

YOUR 401(k) PLAN
How and Where to Invest

Mark L. Schwanbeck

IRWIN
Professional Publishing
Burr Ridge, Illinois
New York, New York

To Judy—

Yes, I really was working, not playing, on my computer.

© RICHARD D. IRWIN, INC., 1994

All rights reserved. No part of this publication may be
reproduced, stored in a retrieval system, or transmitted,
in any form or by any means, electronic, mechanical,
photocopying, recording, or otherwise, without the prior
written permission of the publisher.

This publication is designed to provide accurate and
authoritative information in regard to the subject matter
covered. It is sold with the understanding that neither the
author or the publisher is engaged in rendering legal, accounting,
or other professional service. If legal advice or other expert
assistance is required, the services of a competent professional
person should be sought.

*From a Declaration of Principles jointly adopted by a Committee
of the American Bar Association and a Committee of Publishers.*

Senior sponsoring editor: Amy Hollands Gaber
Project editor: Rita McMullen
Production manager: Ann Cassady
Interior designer: Larry J. Cope
Cover designer: Tim Kaage
Art manager: Kim Meriwether
Compositor: Wm. C. Brown Communications, Inc.
Typeface: 11/13 Palatino
Printer: Arcata/Kingsport

Library of Congress Cataloging-in-Publication Data

Schwanbeck, Mark L.
        Your 401(k) plan: how and where to invest / Mark L. Schwanbeck.
            p.   cm.
        Includes bibliographical references and index.
        ISBN 0–7863–0124–4
        1. 401(k) plans.   2. Employee fringe benefits.   I. Title.
    HF5549.5.C67S385 1994
    332.024'01—dc20   94–2847

Printed in the United States of America

3 4 5 6 7 8 9 0 KP 1 0 9 8 7 6 5 4

Preface

It dawned on me that this book was necessary after one of our company lawyers poked his head in the door of my office one day and said, "Mark, what should I do with my 401(k) plan?" This question has been asked countless times by other employees who needed more information.

Our company doesn't lack for good materials on the 401(k) plan. Every participant gets two booklets and can watch a video presentation when they want to learn more about the plan and its investment offerings. But there is only so much a company can do. After all, our primary business is not publishing material about investing. In addition, our company has a pretty conservative legal department that doesn't want to appear to be giving investment advice. So, to answer the question, "What should I do with my 401(k) plan?" I wrote this book.

This book is written for the average employee who has no investment experience. However, it is not a book on investment advice and strategies. Instead it is a basic look at how a 401(k) plan works and what choices of investments you may have and how to allocate your funds among them. It will discuss specific features of these plans—how and when to withdraw funds, how to take advantage of loans, how to avoid being taxed when changing jobs or retiring, and how to measure the performance of your investment options.

To cover these topics, Chapters 2 through 5 cover the basics of investing to help you with your 401(k) plan investments. Individual retirement accounts (IRAs), estate planning, college savings strategies, and other personal investing topics are covered only as they relate to a 401(k) plan. Chapters 6 and 7 discuss how 401(k) plans work, the tax regulations that affect them, and strategies that you can use to maximize your savings throughout your career. Finally, Chapter 8 discusses strategies for retirement.

Because of the scope of the subject, I have made this book as concise as possible. Whenever you try to simplify complex financial and legal information on investments and taxes, there are bound to be exceptions to the rule, many of which are noted. However, to keep things simple, advanced investment ideas and tax situations that apply to only a few individuals are glossed over or skipped entirely. One of the reference texts I used to write this book has almost 1,000 pages devoted to regulations and laws pertaining to 401(k) plans. Obviously this book can't cover every situation covered by the U.S. tax code.

Thus, a major caveat is in order: Consult with the experts to learn more about your particular situation.

This book should provide you with a basic understanding about how the typical 401(k) plan works. Use this knowledge to ask questions. Nothing can replace the advice of your benefits representative, tax advisor or accountant, or personal financial planner.

As you approach retirement age, you should definitely consult with a tax advisor and financial planner to examine all the issues related to your personal financial situation. The tax structure of the United States makes retirement planning complicated, and you will need more help than one book can provide.

I have made an effort throughout to present investing information as objectively as possible. Your circumstances will determine the correct investment for you. The tables and text will give you an idea of how much and in which investment funds you should invest. None of the information in this book should be interpreted as investment advice. It is presented to help you make your own decisions.

But there is one piece of advice that I must give. Nothing in this book will matter unless you begin saving in your company's 401(k) plan now. Every day that you put off saving costs you the potential to earn money in one of the country's last tax-sheltered investments. *If you haven't done so already, sign up today!* Save as much as you can possibly afford. Every year try to increase the amount you save. While reducing your income today may be painful, you'll appreciate having an adequate amount of money to see you through retirement.

Mark L. Schwanbeck

Acknowledgments

This book could not have been written without the help of many authors whose works I have read and seminar leaders whose speeches I have listened to. All had an impact. In particular, the discussions and ideas of Barbara Nicolich, Mary Stepp, Victor Sidhu, and Jeffrey Paster of Capital Group's American Funds were invaluable in setting the tone of the book.

Patient and kind reviews by Lisa Frieda of Times Mirror, Steve Vernon at the Wyatt Company, and Joe Ross of Merrill Lynch Financial Consultant Training Staff improved the content considerably.

Finally, I would like to thank Amy Gaber at Irwin Professional Publishing for turning the manuscript into the book you are reading today.

Contents

Chapter One

It's Your 401(k) Plan

I t usually starts about a year after you join the company. An envelope arrives from the human resources department inviting you to sign up for the company's 401(k) plan. Specifically, you might be asked to sign up for the Savings Plan, Savings Plus, or possibly the Savings and Profit Sharing Plan. Your company will have its own name for the plan, but the materials you read and the forms you fill out will ask you to set aside money for retirement.

Who me? Retire? I'm only 25 (or 30 or 35 or 40) years old!

Welcome to the world of the 401(k).

Depending on your company's program, you may be invited to a meeting or asked to watch a video explaining what the plan is all about. It's all pretty much a mystery, and your first thought is to put it off. After all, you think, "Do I really want to reduce my paycheck? What's in it for me?"

Or maybe you have been with the company awhile and have forgotten about the 401(k) plan you signed up for. That's easy to do. The plan is pretty convenient, since the funds are deducted from your paycheck before you have a chance to spend it. Most participants get used to a slightly smaller paycheck and don't give the 401(k) plan much thought. But then one day a statement arrives, and you discover that the hundred or so dollars that has been put into the plan every payday has grown to a substantial nest egg.

You wonder: "What should I do with my 401(k) plan? Am I saving enough?" Perhaps you are wondering, "Why can't I withdraw my money and spend it?"

Can You Answer These Questions About Your 401(k) Plan?

- How much should I set aside?
- What investment options are best for me?
- When should I change my investment options?
- How do I change investment options?
- How do I evaluate how well my investments are doing?
- Why don't they let me take out my money when I want it?
- How do I use this plan to save for retirement?
- Is there a catch? Why is the company doing this?
- How much income will I have when I retire and will that be enough?

Or you might ask, "How do I know if my investment choices are doing well?" If you have questions like these, this is the book for you. 401(k) plans are the most popular benefits offered by many companies. Sometimes they seem complicated, but you must make decisions that will ultimately affect your retirement income. *Nobody else can do it for you.*

THE 401(k) PLAN IS FLEXIBLE

Unlike most employer-provided benefits, a 401(k) plan gives you *choice.* In most companies, you have little choice in selecting the medical plan, and other benefits such as life insurance and the defined benefit pension plan are based on fixed formulas that account for years of service and salary. You have little or no control in the management of these benefits.

The 401(k) plan puts the responsibility of managing your savings directly in your control. With that responsibility you get flexibility. You decide:

- How the funds are to be invested.
- How much to save and when to increase or decrease the amount withdrawn from your paycheck. (In hard times you can stop saving entirely and start again when times get better.)

- What investment options to use and how much risk to take to achieve your investment goals.

Although your company will probably help you make your decisions by providing educational materials and seminars, your company is saying to you, "This is your money; you figure out how to invest it." As we will see later, we are not talking about small amounts of money. Someone who is 30 years old could easily accumulate a portfolio worth $500,000 to more than $1 million by retirement.

CONTRIBUTIONS TO THE 401(k) PLAN ARE TAX DEFERRED

A lot of employees like the idea of saving in a 401(k) plan, especially when they see the tax advantages. The U.S. government and most state governments allow your company to deduct your contribution before calculating the income taxes you owe. You still pay Social Security and Medicare taxes on the full amount of your income, but the reduction for U.S. and state income taxes (if allowed) can substantially reduce the tax you pay. An example showing a calculation of the annual benefit appears in the box on page 4.

Most companies will help you make this calculation. Ask your benefits department to help you calculate how much you can save through the 401(k) plan.

Once you have put money into the 401(k) plan, not only do you have the initial savings in taxes, but the entire investment—including capital gains, dividends, and interest—grows tax free. If you had saved the $2,400 shown in the example in a bank savings account or mutual fund, you would have to pay income taxes each year on the interest earned on those savings. The next chapter will show how fast your savings can grow when they are compounded. They will grow even faster when you do not have to pay taxes on the investment earnings each year.

An accountant will tell you that you are merely deferring taxes, not avoiding them. When the funds are withdrawn at retirement, you will have to pay taxes on them. However, at retirement you may be in a lower tax bracket, so the effect may not be as great.

How Much More Will You Save?

Suppose your annual income is $30,000 after paying Social Security and Medicare taxes. Assuming you are filing as a single taxpayer, the federal tax is 15 percent on the first $21,450 and 28 percent on the amount over $21,450. Let's also assume the state where you live adds another 5 percent and also allows you to contribute to a 401(k) plan on a tax-deferred basis. You contribute 8 percent of your wages to the 401(k) plan each year.

	When You Contribute 8% of Income per Year to a 401(k) Plan	When You Do Not Contribute to a 401(k) Plan
Gross income (after Social Security and Medicare taxes)	$30,000	$30,000
401(k) plan contribution (8% of wages)	−2,400	
Taxable Income	$27,600	$30,000
Federal taxes (15%/28%—single taxpayer)	−4,940	−5,612
State taxes (5% per year)	−1,380	−1,500
Total taxes	−$6,320	−$7,112
Spendable income	$21,281	$22,889
How much less do you pay in taxes with the 401(k) plan?	$792	
How much less in spendable income do you have	$1,608	
How much have you saved for your retirement?	$2,400	

In other words, you have saved $2,400, but you have reduced your spendable income by only $1,608. There are very few other ways that you can save $2,400 but pay only $1,608!

One way to look at this tax break is to say that the United States is lending you a portion of the money to invest, and you pay back the loan when you are retired.

There is a caveat concerning the tax break the U.S. government gives you. The tax break is meant to provide you with an incentive to save for retirement. The lawmakers who established the rules governing 401(k) plans recognized that Social Security is not likely to provide you with enough income to live comfortably in retirement. At the same time the tax-deferred features encourage you to save, the rules that govern the 401(k) plan make it very difficult for you to withdraw your funds. Chapter 7 discusses when early withdrawals are permitted and the penalties you may have to pay if you withdraw your money from a 401(k) plan before age 59½.

Pre-Tax versus After-Tax Savings

Many companies give you the choice to save both before and after taxes. The examples in this chapter assume that you are saving pre-tax. This is the best way to save for retirement.

After-tax savings—called voluntary contributions—are permitted so that you can increase your savings beyond what the law allows for pre-tax savings. It is also somewhat easier to withdraw savings from the after-tax account than the pre-tax account, although your investment earnings will still be subject to taxation and penalties.

MANY COMPANIES MATCH YOUR CONTRIBUTION

Many companies help their employees save for retirement by matching a portion of each employee's own contribution. The matching formulas differ by company, and you should find out if and how much your company matches. The matching contribution has a powerful multiplying effect on a 401(k) plan savings.

Let's see what happens to the amount you can save when your company matches your savings:

How Much More Will You Save When the Company Matches Your Contribution?

Using the figures in the previous example, let's assume that for each dollar you contribute your company matches with 50 cents.

	When You Contribute 8% of Income per Year to a 401(k) Plan	When You Do Not Contribute to a 401(k) Plan
Gross income (after Social Security and Medicare taxes)	$30,000	$30,000
401(k) plan contribution (8% of wages)	–2,400	
Taxable Income	$27,600	$30,000
Federal taxes (15%/28%—single taxpayer)	–4,940	–5,612
State taxes (5% per year)	–1,380	–1,500
Total taxes	–$6,320	–$7,112
Spendable income	$21,281	$22,889
Your 401(k) contribution	$2,400	
Company's 50% matching contribution	$1,200	
Total savings	$3,600	

The company match helps you save $3,600 a year, but your spendable income has been reduced by only $1,608.

Another way for you to think about the company's matching contribution is as an instant investment return. In effect, when your company matches 50 percent of your contribution, you have received an immediate 50 percent return on your investment. In the following chapters you will learn that a reasonable long-term expected rate of return is somewhere between 5 and 10 percent per year. When you compare the company's contribution with the 5 to 10 percent annual return you can expect to earn on your investments, it is easy to see what a powerful benefit is being provided.

THE 401(k) PLAN MIGHT BE A SOURCE OF CASH

While the objective of the 401(k) plan is retirement savings, provisions in the law allow companies to provide a loan feature for employees. More than half of 401(k) plans do so. It is an attractive option. While saving for retirement, you can borrow from your plan at favorable interest rates to pay immediate expenses such as college tuition or a down payment on a home. However, there may be problems in borrowing from a 401(k) plan. To decide whether a loan from your plan is right for you, see Chapter 7.

THE 401(k) PLAN IS PORTABLE

Your contributions and earnings in the plan belong to you. They can be moved to another 401(k) plan or an individual retirement account (IRA) when you change jobs. If you are vested in the plan (see Chapter 7 for an explanation of vesting), your company's matching contribution and earnings also belong to you and can be moved to another plan when you change jobs.

Extra savings, lower taxes, loans, and portability. No wonder employees of companies that offer a 401(k) plan usually rank it as one of the most popular company benefits.

YOU ARE IN CHARGE

With a 401(k), you are in charge. The choice to participate is yours. However, you should know that most companies assume you will participate in the 401(k) plan if it is offered. Other retirement income plans, such as a pension plan, provided by the company are probably designed with the assumption that you will invest your own money in the 401(k) plan to supplement the income provided by the other plans.

Your Benefits under the 401(k) Plan

- *Convenient*. Savings are automatic; you are never tempted not to save.
- *Many choices*. A company may offer three or more investment options from which to choose.
- *Tax sheltered*. Savings are sheltered from federal and most state income taxes.
- *Matching*. The company often matches a portion of the contribution.
- *Portable*. Savings can be transferred from company to company or rolled over into an IRA.
- *Loans*. Money may sometimes be borrowed from the plan at attractive interest rates.

Many companies also assume that you will invest responsibly. That means younger employees will use investment options that offer growth potential to enable them to stay ahead of inflation. But the company cannot make you participate in the 401(k) plan or even make you invest in the options that are likely to beat inflation. That is up to you.

In practice, many employees invest conservatively because they are afraid of losing money. Consequently, they contribute wholly to the investment options that have the least price volatility.

BERNIE AND JUDY

Consider the consequences of being too conservative. Bernie, an accountant, knows numbers. Although he hasn't spent much time thinking about investing, he hates the idea of ever losing money. When he sees his 401(k) plan's quarterly statements, he wants to see his account balance grow and *never* decline. Bernie invests in the plan's most conservative option, the guaranteed income fund. It is stable and his principal is guaranteed—or at least Bernie thinks so.

TABLE 1–1
Comparing Retirement Earnings

	Bernie	Judy	Difference
Starting salary	$ 30,000	$ 30,000	None
401(k) contribution	$132,574	$132,574	None
Investment return	$110,821	$372,843	$262,022
Rate of return	4%	8%	4%
Total savings available for retirement	$243,395	$505,417	$262,022

Bernie, who is 30 years old and earns $30,000 a year, expects his salary to grow at the rate of inflation. (Let's ignore the possibility of promotions.) He saves 6 percent of his salary in the 401(k) plan. The most conservative investment option will probably earn about 4 percent per year over the 35 years until Bernie retires. The growth rate will be stable and Bernie will contribute $132,574 toward his retirement. The earnings or return on his investment would be $110,821. His total nest egg at retirement would be $243,395. Not a bad return, right?

But look at Judy, from marketing research. Like Bernie, she is 30 years old, earns $30,000 per year, and is 35 years from retirement. Judy invests 6 percent of her salary and also assumes her salary will grow at the rate of inflation. She investigated all the investment options in the company's 401(k) plan and decided that she was young enough to absorb the risks of the stock market. She chose the company's balanced fund and equity fund options. While these options will have quarterly and annual fluctuations in earnings, over the long run the combination is expected to return 8 percent per year.

Like Bernie, Judy will contribute $132,574. However, the total earnings Judy will achieve under her options are remarkably different. Judy will earn $372,843 for a total retirement nest egg of $505,417—more than twice what Bernie would have at retirement!

Look at Table 1–1 to see the difference the rate of return makes. For Bernie and Judy, 4 percentage points amounts to a $262,022 difference in retirement savings.

WHAT IS THE CATCH?

If you think this sounds too good to be true, you are right. There is a catch. *You face substantial income tax penalties if you take your money out before you are 59½ years old.* For example, if you change jobs and don't roll over (transfer) your account balance into your new employer's 401(k) plan or an IRA, you must pay income taxes at your current rate, plus a 10 percent penalty for early withdrawal. Your state may also assess a penalty tax on the withdrawal. Some hardship rules allow you to withdraw early while still employed *but you must still pay all the ordinary state and federal income taxes and the penalty taxes.* (Chapter 7 will show you how to calculate the effect of withdrawing early and help you decide whether it is the right thing to do.)

Early withdrawal from your 401(k) plan can get complicated. Don't blame your company for the rules. 401(k) plans are regulated by the U.S. government to encourage saving for retirement; your company is simply following the rules.

If you think you are going to need the money in the short term, say within the next five years, you should consider saving in your plan's after-tax option (if the option is available) or invest outside the plan in a mutual fund or bank savings account.

SUMMARY

- 401(k) plans provide you with portability, investment options, and choice. You are in charge.
- They are a great way to save for retirement.
- The U.S. government gives you an immediate tax shelter for 401(k) plan contributions and earnings on your savings.
- The most conservative investment option is not always the best. Consider all your choices.

Chapter Two

Compounding
Making Your Savings Grow

I n Chapter 1 you were introduced to Bernie and Judy and how they saved for retirement. Bernie's investment choice earns a 4 percent return compounded annually, while Judy's choices provide an 8 percent rate of return. Table 1–1 on page 9 shows that Bernie's investment return is $110,821 and Judy's return is $372,843. Both Bernie and Judy are paid the same salary and contribute the same percent of salary to the 401(k) plan; the only difference is the rate of return on their investment and how it compounds over time.

FOUR FACTORS OF INVESTING

Whether you are investing on your own or in the 401(k) plan, four factors must be considered:

1. *Amount.* How much can you afford to invest?
2. *Time.* How long will it take for the investment to pay off?
3. *Rate of Return.* How much do you expect to earn on the investment?
4. *Risk.* What is the likelihood of achieving your expected rate of return during the time you are investing? How much fluctuation in value, that is, volatility, can you tolerate while you are investing?

This chapter covers the first three factors, which make up the components of compounding. Risk will be the subject of the next chapter.

The four factors of investing are generic. This chapter and the next will not discuss 401(k) plans specifically. We will return to 401(k) investing in Chapter 3.

COMPOUNDED RETURN: A SIMPLE DEFINITION

Compounded return is earning money on funds that have already made money for you. The more time you give compounding to work, the more your investments will grow in value.

An example will make compounding easy to understand (see Table 2–1). If you invest $1,000 at the beginning of the year and earn a return of 10 percent, at the end of the year you will have $1,100 in your account—$100 more than you started with. If you also realize a 10 percent return in the second year, your account will have grown to $1,210. You started with $1,110 and earned

TABLE 2–1
Earnings Compounded at 10% Per Year

End of Year	Earnings	Balance
Start with		$1,000.00
1	$100.00	$1,100.00
2	110.00	1,210.00
3	121.00	1,331.00
4	133.10	1,464.10
5	146.41	1,610.51
6	161.05	1,771.56
7	177.16	1,948.72
8	194.87	2,143.59
9	214.36	2,357.95
10	235.79	2,593.74

$110—$10 more than the previous year. By the eighth year you will have doubled your original investment, assuming you can achieve a 10 percent return each year. By the 12th year, you will have tripled the original investment.

In this example, you started with a fixed amount of money and let it grow. In a 401(k) plan, however, you contribute money to your account with each paycheck. Each contribution is compounded from the day it is invested until it is paid out to you.

TIME IS THE FRIEND OF COMPOUNDING

Meet two individuals—Chris and Katherine—for another example of compounding (see Table 2–2). Chris is 25 years old and begins saving $100 a month in the 401(k) plan, or $1,200 a year. Chris's investment options earn 8 percent annually. After 10 years Chris stops investing, but leaves the account untouched until retirement.

Katherine, on the other hand, doesn't begin saving in the 401(k) plan until she is 45 years old. She then saves until retirement at 65. However, for Kathrine to have the same balance at retirement as Chris, she will need to save $332 a month for 20 years. Remember, Chris only had to put aside $100 a month for 10 years.

To achieve the same savings, Chris had to contribute $13,200, while Katherine had to contribute $83,711. The difference is attributed to when they started to save and the amount of time their investments were allowed to grow.

The longer you let your investments compound, the better the results.

CAN A FEW PERCENTAGE POINTS MAKE A DIFFERENCE?

Time is not the only friend of the investor; so is the rate of return. Chapter 3 will explain the relationship between risk and return. Let's assume now that to achieve higher returns you must take

TABLE 2–2
Example of Compounding at an 8% Annual Rate of Return

Age	Chris Annual Contribution	Chris Year-End Balance	Katherine Annual Contribution	Katherine Year-End Balance
25	$ 1,200	$ 1,296		
26	1,200	2,696		
27	1,200	4,207		
28	1,200	5,840		
29	1,200	7,603		
30	1,200	9,507		
31	1,200	11,564		
32	1,200	13,785		
33	1,200	16,184		
34	1,200	18,775		
35	1,200	21,573		
36		23,298		
37		25,162		
38		27,175		
39		29,349		
40		31,697		
41		34,233		
42		36,972		
43		39,929		
44		43,124		
45		46,574	$ 3,986	$ 4,305
46		50,299	3,986	8,955
47		54,323	3,986	13,976
48		58,669	3,986	19,399
49		63,363	3,986	25,256
50		68,432	3,986	31,582
51		73,906	3,986	38,414
52		79,819	3,986	45,792
53		86,204	3,986	53,761
54		93,101	3,986	62,367
55		100,549	3,986	71,661
56		108,593	3,986	81,699
57		117,280	3,986	92,540
58		126,662	3,986	104,248
59		136,795	3,986	116,893
60		147,739	3,986	130,550
61		159,558	3,986	145,299
62		172,323	3,986	161,228
63		186,109	3,986	178,431
64		200,997	3,986	197,011
65		217,077	3,986	217,077
Total contribution	$13,200		$83,706	

FIGURE 2-1
Account Balances after 10 Years at Various Rates of Return

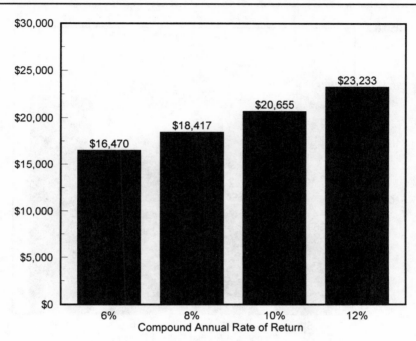

more risk. Frequently, investors in 401(k) plans figure that it isn't worth taking the risk. They ask themselves, "If I can get a relatively safe return at 6 percent, why should I take on additional risk to achieve an 8 percent return? What difference can two additional points make?" A few percentage points in return can make a great difference. If you had invested $100 a month in the 401(k) plan, Figure 2-1 shows how much you would have saved at the end of 10 years at each rate of return, and Figure 2-2 shows how much you would have saved at the end of 25 years at each rate of return.

After 25 years, your account balance with an 8 percent return would be 37 percent more than one earning 6 percent—a difference of $26,092. Two percentage points can make a great deal of difference over time!

FIGURE 2–2
Account Balances after 25 Years at Various Rates of Return

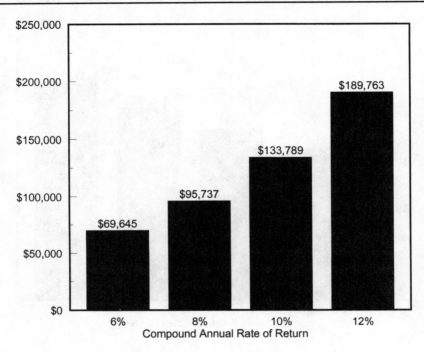

COMPOUNDING WORKS IN BOTH DIRECTIONS

Compounding is simple mathematics. It works in both directions. Suppose you start with a $1,000 investment. In the first year, you earn a return of 10 percent and in the second year you lose 10 percent. Does your investment break even at the end of the second year; that is, are you back to where you started with your $1,000 investment?

The answer is no. You are down by $10 from your original investment. To get back to the $1,100 you had achieved at the end of year 1, you would have to earn a return of 11.1 percent in year 3.

Just as compounding magnifies the return in the positive direction, it also magnifies the loss in the negative direction.

Starting investment	$1,000
10% return in Year 1	+$100
End of year 1 balance	$1,100
10% loss in year 2	−$110
End of year 2 balance	$990
11.1% gain in year 3	+$110
End of year 3 balance	$1,100

THE TWO SOURCES OF RETURN

An investment can provide you with savings growth in two ways: capital appreciation and yield. The combination of these two influences the volatility and likelihood that your investment will achieve your investment goals.

Yield

Yield is the cash flow an investment provides. Investments such as bank certificates of deposit (CDs) and bonds pay interest on a periodic basis. Many stocks pay dividends. The amount of these cash payments divided by the size of your investment determines the yield. The yield is stated as the percent of the investment.

For example, if you buy a bond for $1,000 and receive an interest payment of $100 each year, what is the yield?

$$\text{Yield} = \frac{\text{Interest Payment}}{\text{Amount Invested}} = \frac{\$100.00}{\$1,000.00} = 10\%$$

An interest or dividend payment is cash that cannot be taken away from you. It is yours to invest however you choose. In a 401(k) plan, however, the managers of the funds in which you invest will reinvest the interest and dividend payments in accordance with the objectives of the fund. Thus, the higher the yield of an investment, the higher your expected return.

Capital Appreciation

Capital appreciation is the amount your investment grows over time. Capital appreciation is seldom guaranteed. Instead of capital appreciation there might be capital depreciation, or a decline in the value of your investment. Real estate, stocks, and bonds are all subject to capital appreciation and depreciation.

Like yield, capital appreciation is shown as a percent increase or decrease. If you purchase a stock for $10 and a year later its price increases to $20, its value has appreciated by 100 percent over that year.

Unlike yield, which represents a cash payment, appreciation can be realized only if you sell the security. If your $10 stock rises to $20 and then declines to $15, you have achieved a capital appreciation of only 50 percent on your initial investment. If it later drops back in value to $10, your rate of appreciation is zero.

Some investments obtain all of their return from yield. Bank savings accounts or CDs, money market mutual funds, your 401(k) plan's safety of principal fund, and bonds with less than one year to maturity achieve all of their investment return from yield. In these cases, the words *yield* and *return* are used interchangeably to describe the total return of the fund.

Other investments, such as stocks that pay dividends and bonds that mature beyond one year, will obtain their return from a combination of yield and capital appreciation. For example, if you purchase a stock that pays a cash dividend with a 3 percent yield (the amount of the dividend payment divided by the stock price) and it increases in value by 7 percent, your total return is 10 percent.

Generally speaking, investments that pay interest and dividends are more stable than investments that do not have any yield and obtain all of their return from capital appreciation.

AVOIDING MARKET UPS AND DOWNS: DOLLAR COST AVERAGING

Dollar cost averaging is another powerful friend of employees investing in 401(k) plans. When investing in a 401(k) plan, your company deducts the same contribution from each paycheck. If you are paid weekly, a small amount is taken out each week. If you are paid monthly, the deduction is made each month. These contributions add up over time. Frequent and regular investing of equal dollar amounts enables you to average your investment in any market situation. If you are investing in a stock or bond fund, there will be up-and-down fluctuations in value. Averaging into the fund over time allows you to capture the lows and the highs. Dollar cost averaging means you will never be investing all your money at the top of the market or at the bottom of the market.

Here's an example. Suppose you started in January 1987 to invest $200 each month in your 401(k) plan, which in turn invested in Fidelity's Magellan Fund. Every month you invested another $200 and on the last day of the month your 401(k) plan bought shares of Magellan. By December 31, 1993, your 401(k) plan would have invested $16,800 and purchased 289.457 shares on your behalf.

Your first investment on January 30, 1987, would have purchased 3.635 shares ($200 ÷ $50.02 per share). At Magellan's low point during this period, November 30, 1987, your monthly $200 contribution would have purchased 4.996 shares at $40.03 per share. At the end of the period, December 31, 1993, your one-month purchase would have been 2.823 shares at 70.85 per share. When the price of the fund dropped, you were able to purchase more shares (see Figure 2–3).

The line in Figure 2–3 shows the monthly closing price (left axis) of Fidelity's Magellan Fund. The bars represent how many shares were purchased each month (right axis) with a $200 investment. When the price of the fund's shares fell, the bars increased in height. More shares were purchased when the fund sold at lower prices. When the fund sold at higher prices, the number of shares purchased dropped. Over the seven years, the investment represents an average of all the share prices. Purchasing a fund this way means that you will never make all your investments at a very high or very low price.

By December 31, 1993, your $16,800.00 investment in the shares you purchased would have been worth $18,238.68. The average month-end price for the Magellan Fund from 1987 to 1993 was $59.50 per share. Through dollar cost averaging, your average price would have been $58.04 per share.

Actually, your investment would have done better than this example shows because a mutual fund pays dividends to its investors. In a 401(k) plan, that dividend is reinvested in the fund to

FIGURE 2–3
Fidelity Magellan Fund (Invest $200 at Each Month-End)

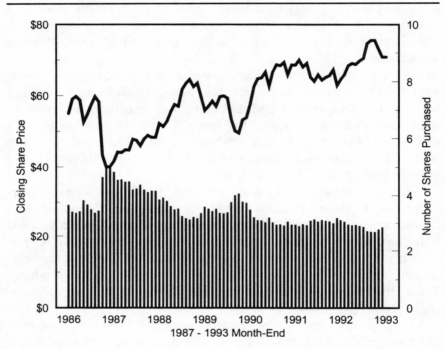

buy more shares. As a result, over the seven years shown in Figure 2–3, you would have accumulated more shares and your invest-ment would have been worth more than $31,000.

SUMMARY

- Compounding is earning a return on money that you have already earned a return on.
- Compounding requires time to have a major impact.
- A difference of a few percentage points can make a huge difference in your total 401(k) plan savings.
- Dollar cost averaging lowers the risk of market timing and is a built-in feature of 401(k) plans.

Chapter Three

Isn't That Risky?

S urveys of 401(k) plan participants show that the most popular investment options are those that are least likely to lose money in any time period. These funds, which go by a variety of names—capital preservation, money market, income, guaranteed income—are often thought to be the least risky. Should you adopt this conservative strategy of investing?

Not always. It is no surprise that preserving capital is the strongest urge for someone starting an investment program. After all, no one likes to lose money. Nevertheless, remember this investing truth: *Investors are paid for taking risk.*

WHAT IS RISK?

If asked, how would you describe an example of risk? Many people mention avoiding an accident of some sort. Others might say they were afraid of losing something, such as their job. To most people risk means that only bad things can happen and risk should be avoided or minimized.

Investment risk is really about the probability of financial success or failure over a particular time period. There is *negative risk*—the probability that the value of investments goes down—and *positive risk*—the probability that the value of investments goes up. Another word that is often used to describe investment risk is *volatility*. A risky investment is likely to be volatile in its price movements.

For example, on any given day, the stock market and investment in stock funds, are very risky. On a day-to-day basis, the stock market is unpredictable. It may go up or down, depending on a variety of factors. However, over a long period of time—a decade or longer—a well-managed and broadly diversified stock fund is a reasonably safe investment and almost certain to increase in value. From the perspective of inflation, many professional investors consider diversified stock funds to be the least risky investment over the long term.

How can one of the riskiest investments on a day-to-day basis become one of the least risky investments over a 10-year time span?

THE RISKS OF INVESTING

Everybody has heard that there is no such thing as a free lunch. It is the same when you invest your savings; there are no risk-free investments. Different types of investments require you to take different kinds of risk. You need to consider several major types of risk when choosing the various options in your 401(k) plan.

Risk 1: Market Risk

Market risk is what most people think of when they say investing in stocks or stock funds is risky. It is created by all the factors that drive the securities markets on a daily basis. Every day we hear on the radio or see in the newspaper that the Dow is up or bonds are down.

Why did the markets move in a particular direction? Many things—political developments, changes in tax law, a large institutional investor buying or selling, rumors among traders, changes in economic indicators such as the Consumer Price Index or employment statistics—can cause the market to rise or fall. Often these market swings are unrelated to the fundamental worth of all the companies that make up the market. The financial markets, like people, can be emotional over the short term and move up or down for seemingly irrational reasons.

The stock market as measured by the Dow Jones Industrial Average, declined by 409 points (about 14 percent) after Iraq invaded Kuwait on August 2, 1990 through January 15, 1991 (see Figure

FIGURE 3–1

Dow Jones Industrial Average from the Invasion of Kuwait to the End of the Persian Gulf War

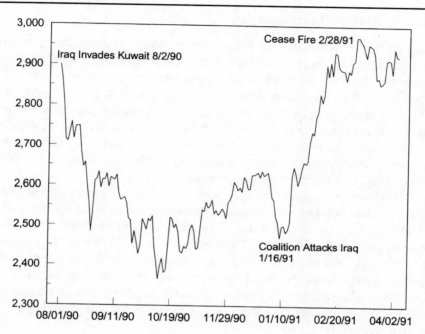

3–1). But on January 16, 1991, when the 28-country coalition began the air attack on Iraq, the market rose by 18 points and recovered all its lost ground by February 28, the day the cease-fire in the Persian Gulf War was announced. *During this time, little changed in the underlying fundamentals of the companies that make up the stock market.* The market's movement was based essentially on the potential for war and its effect on the U.S. economy. To give the market's reaction a human emotion, it was *nervous*. It was asking the question, what if? What if the United States gets into a long war like Vietnam? What if the economy becomes inflationary because of military spending? The market always anticipates the worst when there is uncertainty. Once the bombing of Iraq began and a sense of optimism about the length of the war emerged, the market surged ahead—a form of positive risk.

Risk 2: Business Risk

Over longer periods, the securities markets follow the general movements of the economy. If the economy is in a period of growth, stocks will tend to rise in value as corporate profits increase. At the same time, bonds may decline in value if investors think that the economy is growing too fast and inflation is rising. When the economy levels off and heads into a recession, stocks will usually lose value and the market will enter a "correcting phase." Bonds, on the other hand, might rise in value as interest rates decline and inflationary pressures ease.

Thus, where market risk is a day-by-day or month-to-month factor in the pricing of securities, business risk may affect the markets for a year or two at a time. Figure 3–2 shows stock prices over a long period: January 1, 1970, through January 1, 1993. Recessionary periods are shaded. While not an exact fit, the stock market generally declines during recessions and rises during periods of recovery. The market anticipates the end of a recession and begins to rise before the actual recovery. Likewise, it typically declines before a recession begins.

Risk 3: Inflation Risk

One of the least considered investing risks is *inflation;* that is, the rising prices for goods and services that you buy every day. Let's consider the safest form of investing—doing nothing. What if you placed all of your savings in a bank safe deposit box? The money in the safe deposit box does not gain interest, but it is absolutely safe. (In all the bank failures in this country bank customers have been able to retrieve the contents of their safe deposit boxes.)

If you are risk adverse, what is the harm in saving in this ultraconservative manner? Answer: Inflation. If you placed $1,000 in a safe deposit box on January 1, 1980, that $1,000 would purchase only $518 worth of goods in 1993. Inflation cut your purchasing power by nearly half in the 13 years from 1980

FIGURE 3–2
S&P 500 Index Prices 1970–1992

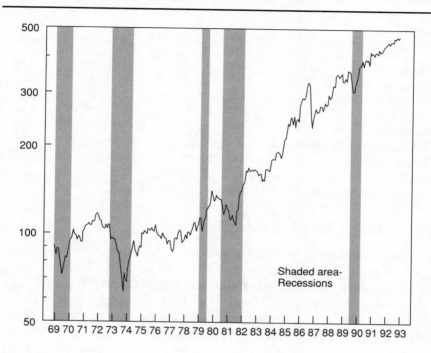

to 1993. To have the same purchasing power as the $1,000 in 1980, you would need almost $2,000 in 1993.

To beat inflation, and simply break even, you would have had to invest the $1,000 and earn a little more than 5 percent each year. Putting your money in a safe deposit box will not protect you from the risk of losing purchasing power to inflation.

Table 3–1 shows how prices increased over one 20-year period. In 1968, one dollar bought almost three gallons of gasoline. Two decades later, one dollar bought slightly over one gallon. Today, you cannot buy a whole gallon for the same dollar.

In order to protect your purchasing power when you retire and avoid inflation risk, you will have to find investments that grow faster than inflation.

TABLE 3–1
How Some Prices Changed from 1968 to 1988

Item	1968 Price	1988 Price	Percent Increase
One gallon of gas	$ 0.34	$ 0.95	179
Box of corn flakes	0.24	1.16	383
Half gallon of milk	0.45	0.93	107
1 lb. of bacon	0.69	1.79	160
McDonald's hamburger	0.15	0.65	334
Full size Plymouth automobile	2,995.00	12,000.00	301
Average income	8,633.00	29,896.00	246

Source: Statistical Abstract of the United States

Risk 4: Security Selection Risk

An individual stock or bond is subject to the market's view of how the company that issued the security will perform. If the majority of investors who make up the market believe that the prospects for increased profits are good, the stock and bond prices of the company will increase. If the company's prospects are not good, the price of its stocks and bonds will decline.

The fluctuations in price also are affected by market and business risk factors. For example, if the market anticipates a recession and the entire stock market declines in price, the value of a specific company may not decline as much because its prospects in a recession are regarded as better than other companies. A few companies in the market usually go against the trend and increase in value during a recession.

The way to minimize security selection risk is to create a portfolio. A *portfolio* is a group of securities. A portfolio manager buys from 10 or 20 to more than a 100 securities to minimize the risk that any one security will do poorly and hurt the entire portfolio. The saying, "Don't put all your eggs in one basket," applies to portfolio management.

All of the investment options in your 401(k) plan, except the company stock fund (shares in the company you work for), will be invested in a portfolio of securities to minimize security selection risk.

RISK WORKS BOTH WAYS

Remember that investment professionals recognize risk as neither all positive nor all negative. Risk works in both directions because what is really being measured is price volatility. The higher the risk of an investment, the more volatile its price and the greater potential for a gain or loss. When constructing a portfolio of investments, the professional will diversify the holdings to balance the risk and the return. You should do the same.

In a 401(k) plan, you can control risk through the process of asset allocation. Allocating your savings among several different funds will help you achieve the amount of risk you can tolerate while maximizing your potential return. To minimize the four types of risk, think about allocating your investments in the following ways:

- **Market risk is controlled through the length of time that you invest.** The longer you invest, the lower your market risk. Over short time periods, market risk can be controlled through the use of the more conservative investment options provided by your 401(k) plan.

- **Inflation risk is minimized through the use of stocks.** Historically, stock prices have grown faster than inflation, so having a part of your 401(k) plan in the funds that purchase stocks will help you beat inflation.

- **Business risk is minimized through the use of bonds with a variety of maturities.** Investing in an actively managed stock fund—where managers make decisions on which stocks to buy and how many shares to hold—may increase the chances that some of the stocks will do better than others during recessions because they are either "recession-proof" or because they tend to do better during downturns.

- **Security Selection Risk is minimized by using several funds that the 401(k) plan offers.** Usually you are exposed to large amounts of security selection risk only when you concentrate your savings in the company stock fund.

Remember, you can minimize risk, but you cannot eliminate it altogether, Even a well-diversified portfolio of market-valued securities of stocks or bonds will still have some risk and fluctuate in value over the short term.

FIGURE 3–3
Risk versus Return of Typical Investments Compared with Inflation,
1926–1992

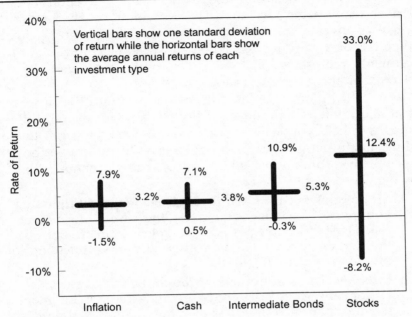

Source: Ibbotson Associates.

MEASURING RISK

Risk can be measured. One popular way of measuring risk is to
calculate the average annual return of an investment and measure
how much the returns fluctuate around the average. The result of
this calculation is the standard deviation. Calculating standard deviation requires the use of statistics and is best left to the professionals. But understanding the result is fairly simple.

Figure 3–3 shows the average returns for stocks, bonds, and
cash compared with the rate of inflation. Here's how to read the
chart. The average annual return for stocks from 1926 through
1992 was 12.4 percent. The standard deviation over that 66-year
period was 20.6 percent. This means that in 68 percent of the years
(45 years) the stock market return, was between the average return of 12.4 percent plus or minus 20.6 percent. Thus, if the future

TABLE 3–2
The Stock Market: Risks and Returns, Various Periods

	Average Annual Return (%)	Standard Deviation (%)
1926–1993 (67 years)	12.4	20.6
1974–1993 (20 years)	13.9	15.9
1979–1993 (15 years)	16.3	12.1
1984–1993 (10 years)	15.5	11.8
1989–1993 (5 years)	15.3	13.6

is like the past, there is a 68 percent chance in any year of achieving a stock market return somewhere between 33.0 percent and –8.2 percent.

This measure shows only a 68 percent chance; in 32 percent of the years, returns could fall outside this range. For example, the best stock market return between 1926 and 1992 was 54 percent in 1933 and the worst return was –43 percent in 1931.

Knowing the standard deviation of a particular investment allows you to compare its risk with that of another investment.

Intermediate bonds (average maturity of five to eight years), for example, have a much lower average rate of return, 5.3 percent, and a lower standard deviation, 5.6 percent, than stocks. Large positive or negative returns are much less likely; thus, intermediate bonds are considered less risky. Notice that the average returns for intermediate bonds are much lower than stocks. Investors in stocks are, in effect, being paid for taking risk.

One of the key assumptions in this type of analysis is that historical returns and risk measurements can be used to predict long-term future returns in the market. While there are no strong arguments against using these returns to make predictions about the future, you should be aware that for periods of 5, 10, and 15 years, returns can be considerably different from the long-run averages. As a result, risk over short periods can be higher or lower than risk over very long periods.

Over the last 20 years, the risk of the stock market, as measured by standard deviation, has been less than the 67-year history of the market. In addition, the returns from the market have been higher during shorter periods. The question is will the market return to the longer-run historical averages or is there a new, higher average return and lower risk? No one knows the answer, but the question spurs a great deal of debate among investment professionals.

In the next chapter, the various types of 401(k) investments are discussed. Returns will be given for shorter periods to show typical variations from the average return. Ultimately, when you consider these investments, you need to evaluate how much risk you can tolerate for the return you expect over the length of time you will be investing in your 401(k) plan.

SUMMARY

- Risk must be considered in every investment decision.
- Risk can be either positive or negative.
- There are four major kinds of risk: market risk, business risk, inflation risk, and security selection risk.
- Diversification reduces the risk of investing.
- Risk can be measured with a technique called standard deviation.

Chapter Four

Your 401(k) Plan's Investment Options

Y ou read in the first three chapters that picking the right investment options from the choices offered by your company's
401(k) plan can make a significant difference in the amount of
money available when you retire. This chapter examines typical
investment options offered by 401(k) plans, and their risks and
rewards.

A survey conducted in 1992 by the Wyatt Company, an employee benefits consulting firm that helps many companies in the
operation of 401(k) plans, indicated that two-thirds of 401(k) plans
have three or more investment options. The range of investment
options runs from one—a company stock fund—to more than 20.

While it is impossible to cover all possible investment options,
this chapter explains how an investment option works and describes the rewards and risks of investing in the five most commonly offered funds found most frequently in 401(k) plans. These
are the safety of principal fund, the bond fund, the equity fund,
the balanced fund, and the company stock fund. After these funds
are discussed, several specialty funds will be described. Your company may call the funds in its 401(k) plan by different names.
Look at the description in your company's 401(k) materials and
prospectus and compare them with the descriptions in this book.

HOW AN INVESTMENT OPTION WORKS

When you invest in a 401(k) plan investment option, what are you
really investing in? Your company takes your contribution and
pools it with the contributions of other employees. The company

hires a portfolio manager to manage the entire fund or invests the pool of money in a mutual fund or collective fund managed by a bank or insurance company. The mutual fund or collective fund used by your 401(k) plan will have investment objectives similar to the fund offered by your company. While there are technical differences between the method your company chooses to invest the assets of the 401(k) plan, with all methods, an investment specialist—a portfolio manager—will manage your contributions.

SAFETY OF PRINCIPAL FUND

Nearly all 401(k) plans offer a fund that provides the participants with safety of principal. The investment objective of the fund is no loss on your contribution. If you invest $1,000, you will get $1,000 back, plus interest on the investment. As close as possible, the safety of principal fund mimics the behavior of a bank certificate of deposit (CD).

With this conservative investment objective, the market risk of this type of fund is negligible. However, as discussed in the last chapter, it is not entirely risk free.

When choosing an investment strategy for the safety of principal fund, your company does everything it can to eliminate the fluctuations in your account balance. Your statement should show that your account balance has increased from the previous period by the amount of your contributions plus whatever interest rate the fund is currently earning. There are two popular types of safety of principal funds: the money market fund and the insurance contract fund.

What is your Safety of Principal Fund called? Typical names include:

Income Fund

Guaranteed Income Fund

Money Market Fund

Cash Fund

Insurance Contract Fund

Money Market Funds

A money market fund invests in debt securities that will mature within one year. When the portfolio manager purchases a debt security, the fund is lending money to a borrower. In return, the borrower promises to pay the fund the principal (i.e., the amount of the investment) plus interest, over a specified period of time. Interest payments are made at regular intervals, typically quarterly, semiannually, or annually. For this reason, debt securities are also called fixed-income securities.

Money market funds are very safe and very liquid. Investors in a money market fund *outside* a 401(k) plan can withdraw their money at any time. Many money market mutual funds provide their investors with a checkbook to make withdrawals just like a bank checking account. Because of their liquidity and low level of market risk, money market funds are considered the equivalent of cash among professional investors.

A large part of most money market fund portfolios are investments in U.S. Treasury bills and other securities guaranteed by the U.S. government. In addition, these funds invest in high-quality corporate securities and bank CDs. By limiting the investments to those that mature within one year and by limiting the average maturity of all the investments in the fund to 120 days or less, money market fund managers ensure that the value of the investment remains constant. The principal should not fluctuate in price. As a result, the money market fund will provide safety of principal in nearly all market conditions. Only in extremely rare circumstances, when interest rates rise rapidly over a very short time, could these funds suffer a slight loss in principal. These conditions so far have never occurred in the U.S. financial markets.

These funds face two more likely types of risk. Because they invest in corporate securities, there is always the risk that a corporation that issues debt will enter bankruptcy and its securities will become worthless. Again, this is an extremely rare occurrence in money market funds because they invest only in high-quality corporate debt. However, in order to be extra cautious, some 401(k) plans invest in money market funds that buy only U.S. government debt, thus eliminating the risk of corporate defaults.

Inflation is the second and by far the largest risk of these funds. Since the losses and price fluctuations on the securities in a money market portfolio are very rare, the market risk is very low. *Low risk translates into low return.*

A money market fund will earn interest that is generally quite close to the rate of inflation. From time to time, the rate of return may even be less than inflation. Figure 3–3 on page 28 shows the 20-year returns of money market funds compared with stocks and bonds.

Guaranteed Investment Contracts

In order to increase the interest rate provided by their safety of principal investment option, many companies purchase investment contracts offered by insurance companies. The insurance industry has marketed these products as *guaranteed investment contracts* (GICs). A few banks offer a similar product called *bank investment contracts* (BICs). (Since GICs and BICs work in the same way, for simplicity the following discussion will refer only to GICs.)

When the 401(k) plan invests in a GIC, it is lending money to an insurance company. In return, the insurance company promises to pay interest on the loan and return the principal at some point, usually within five years.

The insurance company invests the money from the 401(k) plan in securities that will earn more than the interest rate it has promised to pay the 401(k) plan over the life of the contract. By earning more on its investments than it pays the plan, the insurance company makes a profit.

As part of the contract arrangement, the insurance company promises to pay participants their principal plus interest whenever a participant withdraws money from the fund. This feature, which is called *benefit responsive,* enables the insurance company to maintain the constant principal value of the fund, according to current accounting rules.

To provide a more attractive rate of return than the money market funds, the insurance company must take more market risk with the funds it received from the 401(k) plans. The insurance company is required by law to maintain a surplus of assets. Therefore, any

Where Are Insurance Contracts Traded?

Unlike all the other investment options offered by your 401(k) plan, there is no public market for insurance contracts. Each contract is a private transaction between the insurance company and your plan. The insurance carrier considers the circumstances of your plan—number of likely withdrawals, other types of investment options you have, and the probability of participants switching among funds—before making a bid to the fund's portfolio manager. The portfolio manager will usually seek several bids from different carriers to get the best possible interest rate. Because these are private negotiations, there is no public market in contracts. Your fund cannot sell it to another investor. Once the 401(k) plan has purchased a contract, it usually faces penalties for trying to cash out the contract before the maturity date.

daily fluctuations in the price of the securities it purchases have little effect on the insurance company's ability to return principal and interest to the 401(k) plan so that the plan may accommodate a participant's withdrawal request. If the insurance company is careful, the extra return received from the investments more than offsets any short-term fluctuations in their price. As a result, the surplus will grow over time and the insurance company will be profitable.

Like a money market fund, GICs have two principal sources of risk. The guarantee provided by insurance companies is only as good as the institutions providing the guarantee. The insurance company has to be in business when the contract matures! Infrequently, insurance companies make risky investments and become insolvent; they cannot pay contract holders interest payments or principal when the contracts mature. When this happens, the 401(k) plan becomes one of the creditors of the insurance company. It may take years before the plan's fund receives all or even a portion of its investment back.

In 1991, 401(k) plans that purchased contracts from First Executive Life Insurance of California and Mutual Benefit Life Insurance Company of New Jersey found themselves in this position.

Questions to Ask About Your Insurance Fund

Is the insurance fund diversified among many carriers? How many? (For large funds, there should be five to ten carriers.)

What is the average size of an insurance contract within the fund? (Depending on the fund size, a contract should represent about 5 percent of the fund's assets.)

What is the average credit quality of the insurance carriers represented in the fund? What is the worst credit quality rating? (A good average quality for a fund is AA, with no insurance carrier rated below A or A–.)

Are any insurance carriers in the fund in danger of defaulting on the plan's contracts? Have any defaulted in the past?

Does the fund use synthetic GICs or market-valued securities to increase the diversification?

The underlying portfolio of First Executive Life was invested in below investment grade, high-yield corporate bonds, which are commonly called *junk bonds*. The high-yield bond market is volatile and subject to large price fluctuation. In 1990, when the high-yield market declined, First Executive Life's surplus was not adequate to cover the losses on its investments and the demands of its contract holders. The company was taken over by the State of California.

Mutual Benefit Life faced a similar situation. Its underlying investments were invested in real estate. When the value of real estate declined in 1990 and 1991, it didn't have enough surplus to pay policyholders and contract holders.

In both cases, the 401(k) plans that hold contracts from these insurance companies will probably receive all or a large portion of their investment back. But the payoff will be made much later than expected, and the 401(k) plan participants have to wait to get even a portion of their funds. Participants who are years away from retirement are losing the compounding power of the funds tied up in contracts with Executive Life and Mutual Benefit. The problems with First Executive Life and Mutual Benefit Life caused many companies that sponsor 401(k) plans to look for other ways to diversify the assets within their safety of principal funds.

Synthetic GICs. A variation on the GIC in safety of principal funds is the *synthetic GIC.* In order for the company to assure its employees that negative price fluctuations are nearly impossible and still achieve returns higher than money market funds, a new product has been created. The company hires a portfolio manager to invest in limited-maturity bonds (see the next section) and notes. This will help the 401(k) plan achieve higher returns. At the same time, the company buys a contract from an insurance company or bank that guarantees that the employees can withdraw their money at any time and get back all of their contributions plus any interest paid on those contributions. It is really like buying automobile or homeowners insurance to protect yourself from a catastrophe. If the fund does well over a period of time, the plan can easily accommodate withdrawals by paying its participants principal plus interest. If the bond market declines, the insurance company makes up the difference between the market value of the investments and what is owed to participants requesting withdrawals. Even though the insurance company does not manage the assets, it guarantees the principal.

With a synthetic GIC, if the insurance carrier enters bankruptcy, all the 401(k) loses is its guarantee. The plan still owns all the assets that are invested by the portfolio manager in limited-maturity, fixed-income securities.

While this may sound like the best of both worlds—a well-diversified portfolio, plus a principal guarantee—these insurance contracts tend to reduce the returns of a safety of principal portfolio by ¼ to ½ percentage point per year. This can be a significant reduction in return when safety of principal funds are returning only 3 to 4 percent per year and only marginally staying ahead of inflation.

Limited-Maturity Bond Funds

One approach that companies use in addition to GICs or BICs is to invest in limited-maturity bonds. *Limited-maturity bonds* are similar to the investments made by money market funds except that they mature within three years instead of one. As a result, they are subject to market risk and price fluctuations. However, when limited-maturity bonds are mixed with insurance contracts, the negative fluctuations in price can be almost eliminated. In a portfolio

What Is an Index?

Professional investment managers can gauge their performance by looking at an index of securities similar to the portfolio they are managing. For example, the manager of a bond fund might compare the fund's performance with the Lehman Brothers Aggregate Index (LB-AGG). The LB-AGG includes all the U.S. government, U.S. agencies, investment-grade corporate bonds, and mortgage securities that are available at any point in time. In 1993, it included more than 6,000 issues worth more than $3.9 trillion. As the price of the LB-AGG changes, a portfolio manager can determine whether his or her portfolio is doing better or worse than the bond market.

There are hundreds of indexes available to measure the performance of the stock and bond markets.

that contains 50 percent limited-maturity bonds and 50 percent GICs, the probability of a decline in principal is nearly zero over any period longer than six months. By diversifying the portfolio with limited-maturity bonds, the 401(k) plan cuts its exposure to insurance contracts while preserving its goal of safety of principal.

BOND FUNDS

Many 401(k) plans offer their participants a bond fund, which is similar to money market and limited-maturity bond funds. The difference is that bond funds will invest in the debt securities of the U.S. government, U.S. agencies, and corporations, with maturities as long as 30 years. The longer the maturity of the bond, the greater the market risk and the likelihood of price fluctuations. At the same time, longer maturity usually means higher interest rates and greater long-term returns.

There is an active market for bonds, which are traded daily in the world's financial centers. Generally speaking, the price of a bond is affected primarily by interest rate trends and the investors' view of the stability of the issuer. As interest rates decline, bond prices rise—and vice-versa. Likewise the better the credit standing of the issuer, the lower the interest payments its bonds will pay. In the U.S.

TABLE 4–1
Types of Bond Funds and Periods of Negative Returns

	Type of Bond Fund			
	Cash Equivalent	*Short Maturity*	*Intermediate Maturities*	*Very Long Maturities*
	Representative Index			
	91-Day Treasuries	*Merrill Lynch 1–3 Treasuries*	*Lehman Aggregate*	*Lehman Long-Term Bonds*
Five-Year Comparisons 1988–1992 (60 months)				
Negative return months	0	7	14	18
Negative return quarters	0	0	2	3
Negative return years	0	0	0	0
Ten-Year Comparisons 1983–1992 (120 months)				
Negative return months	0	15	30	40
Negative return quarters	0	0	5	7
Negative return years	0	0	0	1

fixed-income market, the U.S. government has the highest credit rating. Therefore, Treasury bonds and bonds guaranteed by the U.S. government pay the lowest interest rates at any point in time.

Corporate bonds pay higher interest rates than U.S. Treasury bonds. The amount of interest payment depends on the credit rating of the company issuing the bonds. As the credit standing of a corporation improves, it pays lower interest rates for its bonds than bonds of the same maturity issued by a corporation with a lower credit rating.

The typical bond fund found in a 401(k) plan is considered an *intermediate bond fund,* one in which the average maturity of all the securities in the fund ranges from five to eight years. This fund typically invests in a combination of U.S. government securities, U.S. agency securities, mortgage-backed bonds, and corporate bonds.

Table 4–1 shows the risk of having a negative month for various types of bond funds. For the most part, all bond funds, except those with very long maturities, will be more stable and less risky than the equity funds discussed in the next section.

EQUITY FUNDS

If you buy a stock, you become part owner of a business. If you invest in a fund that buys stocks, you become a part owner of many businesses. Stocks are a form of investment known as *equity*, which means ownership interest.

Although you are one of thousands of owners of the companies in which your equity fund invests, you face many of the same opportunities and problems faced by any owner of a business. When a business does well, the value of the company increases, its stock price increases, and your fund goes up in value. If the company loses a contract or is having a difficult time because of a recession, the value of the company declines and its stock price drops. Since the economy is constantly moving through cycles of ups and downs, businesses and their stocks constantly fluctuate in value. However, as long as the country's economy grows, the majority of stocks that make up the market generally rise over time.

It takes patience to ride out the part of the cycle when stocks decline. Bear markets, which are broad declines in the stock market, can last several years. But, if you do not need to use your savings for five to ten years, the rewards of investing in the stock market are well worth the volatility.

Figure 4–1 illustrates how well money market securities, bonds, and stocks—as represented by an index appropriate to each market—have performed over the past 20 years on an average annual basis compared with inflation. It shows why financial planners advise their clients to put part of their assets in stocks. Over the long term, stocks provide the maximum return compared with bonds and money market securities. They are the best investments to achieve capital appreciation and beat inflation.

FIGURE 4–1
Market Returns 1979–1993 (Annualized Returns)

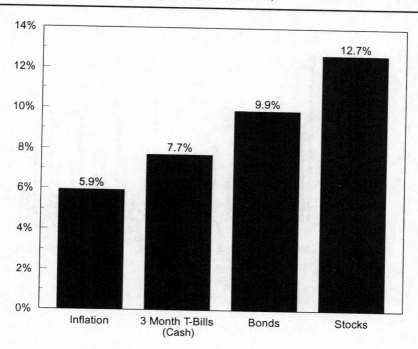

Figure 4–2 shows the return of the Standard & Poor's (S&P) 500 Index for each year since 1949. Over this 45-year period, stocks have increased in 35 years and declined in only 10. While you should be wary of using past market performance to predict future results, the graph gives you a picture of how stock returns fluctuate. Only once did the market have two negative years in a row. When the market increased in value, the average annual return was 20 percent; in the years it declined, the market lost 10 percent. The average return for all years was 14 percent.

The S&P 500 Index returns are usually considered representative of the entire stock market (see Table 4–2). Based on market capitalization, the S&P 500 Index includes the 500 largest companies

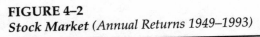

FIGURE 4–2
Stock Market (Annual Returns 1949–1993)

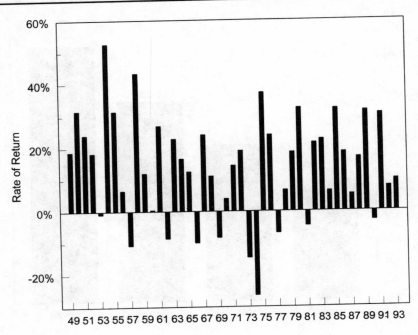

actively trading on the New York and American Stock Exchanges, and in the over-the-counter (OTC) market. Together the 500 stocks in the index represent about 70 percent of the value of all the stocks trading in the United States. Your 401(k) plan probably has an equity fund that offers similar results. There are two types of these broadly diversified equity funds—actively managed funds and passively managed funds.

Active Equity Management

When a portfolio is actively managed, the portfolio manager will buy stocks in concentrations that are different from the benchmark. If the portfolio's benchmark is the S&P 500 Index, the manager could simply purchase all 500 stocks in the index in the same proportion as the index. Excluding the administration costs, the

TABLE 4–2
S&P 500 Index Average Annual Returns

Summary of the best, worst, and average 5-, 10-, and 15-year periods over the 50 years through 1990.

	5 Years	10 Years	15 Years
Best	+23.9%	+20.1%	+18.2%
Worst	−2.4%	+1.2%	+4.3%
Average	+12.4%	+11.9%	+11.4%

portfolio should return an amount equal to the return of the index. However, an active manager will try to beat the index and provide a higher return. Through analysis of stocks, sectors of the market, and the economy, the portfolio manager will buy a portfolio of stocks that have different characteristics compared to the index. For example, suppose the portfolio manager believes that consumers are going to cut spending over the next year. When purchasing stocks for the portfolio, the manager will underweight retail stocks. If the manager is right and the prices of retail stocks decline due to poor sales, the portfolio will outperform the benchmark which continues to hold retail stocks.

The manager also tries to reduce the volatility of the entire portfolio relative to the benchmark. Most 401(k) plans with an actively managed U.S. equity fund option use the S&P 500 Index as their benchmark (see box on page 44).

Doing better than an index is sometimes difficult. During the 10 years through the end of 1992, only about 30 percent of the equity funds monitored by Morningstar, an organization that monitors the performance of more than 2,700 mutual funds of all types, were able to beat the S&P 500 Index.

Passive Equity Management

Passively managed funds or index funds attempt to replicate the target index's investment return and volatility. Index funds are considered to be passively managed because there is no research

---

Typical Stock Indexes

The **Standard & Poor's 500 Index** is the most popular of the U.S. stock market indexes among professional investors. This index is comprised of 500 stocks from 83 industrial groups. It represents the aggregate market value of all the shares of the index's 500 companies, or about $3 trillion in 1993.

The **Dow Jones Industrial Average,** sometimes called just "the Dow," represents the average share price of 30 large industrial "blue chip" companies. Dating from 1882, it is the most quoted index and is usually mentioned on the evening television news. The Dow Jones Industrial Average represents a little more than 1 percent of the stocks traded on the New York Stock Exchange. However, despite the small number of stocks and the lack of transportation and utility stocks, its total return has been close to the S&P 500 Index and other broad measures of the stock market over the long run.

Other indexes that are frequently quoted include:

The **Wilshire 5000 Index**—the aggregate value of 5,000 stocks, or nearly all the publicly traded stocks in the United States.

The **Russell 2000 Index**—the aggregate value of the 2,000 smallest companies in the Russell 3000 Index. This index is frequently used as the benchmark for companies with small market capitalizations.

The **Morgan Stanley/Capital International Europe, Australia, Far East Index** (MSCI EAFE) represents more than 1,000 non-U.S. companies in 18 countries, the developed markets of the world outside of the United States.

The **Morgan Stanley/Capital International World Index** (MSCI World) adds the United States and Canada to the EAFE index. It represents nearly 1,500 companies in the world's developed markets with an aggregate market value of $5.5 trillion.

---

required. The manager of the fund simply buys all the stocks in the index. In most cases, this means trying to match the risk and return of the S&P 500 Index. An S&P 500 Index fund purchases all 500 stocks used in the index and holds each in the same proportion.

Critics of passively managed funds argue that it is silly to buy 500 stocks simply because they are in an index. For example, why buy stocks of companies that are likely candidates for bankruptcy? Proponents of passive management argue that index funds provide more than enough diversification so that the performance of any one stock matters little and that an index such as the S&P 500 provides an accurate reflection of the U.S. economy's prospects for growth. Further, they contend, passively managed funds have much lower expenses than actively managed funds, because portfolio managers do not have to research and analyze the prospects of the companies they are buying.

Although professionals continue to debate the merits of active versus passive management of funds, your investment in the equity fund option of your 401(k) plan will, in general, give you a return similar to that of the broad stock market. Companies may call their equity fund option by a variety of names, so look at the materials provided by your company for the fund that compares to the Standard & Poor's 500, the Russell 1000 or 3000, or the Wilshire 5000 Index. This will be the fund that attempts to capture the return of the broad market.

It is important to differentiate the broad equity market fund from other equity options that may involve higher investment risk. The section on specialty funds will describe several other types of equity funds (see page 48).

BALANCED FUND

Another popular investment option available in the 401(k) plans of many companies is the balanced fund, in which the portfolio manager invests in a combination of stocks, bonds, and money market securities. The stocks provide the portfolio with growth and the potential for capital appreciation while the debt securities help dampen some of the price volatility of the stocks and add to the yield of the fund.

Passive versus Active Management

Like the equity funds, balanced funds can be passively or actively managed. When they are passively managed, the materials provided by your company will indicate the percentage of stocks, bonds, and money market securities that the fund holds. A typical ratio might be 60 percent stocks, 30 percent bonds, and 10 percent money market securities. The stock portion of the balanced fund might be invested in an S&P 500 Index Fund, the bond portion in a Lehman Brothers Government/Corporate or Aggregate Index Fund, and the remainder in a money market fund.

Passively managed balanced funds seldom change the allocation among funds. Whenever the ratio of stocks, bonds, and cash changes, the fund is rebalanced to achieve the target ratio. For example, in a fund targeted at 50 percent stocks and 50 percent bonds, if the stock market rises so that the value of stocks represents 55 percent of the fund's total assets, the portfolio manager will sell stocks and buy bonds to bring the ratio back to 50:50.

In actively managed balanced funds, portfolio managers gain a powerful tool. They can change the asset allocation of the funds. For example, when stocks are considered overvalued, they can reduce the holdings of stocks and add more bonds to the investment mix. Your company will provide a description of the balanced fund, the target asset allocation, and the weight that the portfolio manager might give to stocks and bonds in the best- and worst-case situations.

The *target asset allocation* of the balanced fund represents the long term objective for risk and return. For example, over the long run a fund's asset allocation might be 60 percent stocks and 40 percent bonds. This particular combination should result in capturing much of the growth of the stock market while dampening some of the volatility that stocks provide. When the portfolio managers of this balanced fund believe that stocks and bonds are appropriately valued relative to each other, they will set the asset allocation at the target asset allocation. A typical target asset allocation might be 70 percent stocks/30 percent bonds, 60 percent stocks/40 percent bonds, or 50 percent stocks/50 percent bonds.

In a fund with a target asset allocation of 50 percent stocks/50 percent bonds, for example, the portfolio manager might estimate that stocks had become overvalued and reduce the percentage of stocks to 40 percent, while increasing the percentage of bonds to 60 percent. If the stock market declines, the portfolio manager will have eliminated some of the portfolio's losses. That explains why balanced funds that perform well over a long period of time have fewer negative return years than stock funds.

On the other hand, balanced funds never get the returns a pure stock fund achieves because a certain percentage of the portfolio is always held in bonds. Less risk, less reward.

It is also important to recognize that balanced funds reduce volatility but do not eliminate it. Because stock and bond markets move up and down, a balanced fund is still likely to have months, quarters, and a few years with negative returns over the long term.

COMPANY STOCK FUND

If you work for a company that has publicly traded stock, you probably also have the choice of investing in the company stock fund. This investment option buys and sells only company stock. In many 401(k) funds, a company that matches a portion of your contribution does so through the company stock fund. You also may have the option of allocating a portion or all of your contributions to the company stock fund.

Many employees invest a portion of their contributions in the company stock fund. They believe in the prospects for the company and wish to show their support. However, a warning is in order.

The company stock fund, over time, will probably be the most volatile investment option offered in your 401(k) plan.

Any one stock, no matter what company, will be more volatile than the diversified portfolio of stocks in the equity fund option. The reason is simple. When one of the numerous stocks in an equity fund goes up in value, another may go down. Although the portfolio will move in the general direction of the market, portfolio diversification provides a buffer against the whipsaw action that individual stocks undergo.

Individual stocks will rise and fall in value for a variety of reasons. Unexpectedly good earnings may cause the stock to rise by two or three dollars a share in a day or two. Likewise, if the earnings report is below expectation, the stock may decline in value by the same amount. The other stocks that make up the market may not move at all during that time.

TABLE 4–3
Summary Comparison of 401(k) Plan Funds

Type of Fund	Market Risk How likely am I to lose money over short periods (one month to one quarter) of time?	Inflation Risk How likely am I to lose purchasing power over long periods of time?	Expected Long-Term Return
Safety of principal (money market, GIC Funds)	Very low	Very high	Low
Bond fund	Low	Moderate	Moderate
Balanced fund	Moderate	Low to moderate	Moderate
Stock fund (U.S. only)	High	Low	High
Specialty stock funds	Very high	Very low	High
Company stock fund	Very high	Low	Moderate to high

This doesn't mean that investing in the company stock fund is a bad idea. In many cases, a company provides a matching contribution to your plan with company stock. This allows you to participate in the growth of the company that you work for. However, if you receive company stock through the matching contributions, it is probably not a good idea for most 401(k) participants to increase these holdings through your own contributions. As a rule of thumb, many financial planners suggest that you limit your holdings in the company stock fund to no more than 10 or 20 percent of all your savings.

SPECIALTY FUNDS

Most of the funds offered in your plan have probably been described. Wyatt Associates' study of 401(k) plans concluded that if your plan offers only three investment options, they are likely to be the safety of principal, equity, and company stock funds. If you have more investment options, chances are you have the choice of

---

Small Capitalization versus Large Capitalization Funds

Capitalization refers to the value of all the shares of a company that are traded on the stock market. A company with 100 million shares outstanding that sells for $50 per share, will have a capitalization of $5 billion (100,000,000 shares times $50 per share).

There is no single definition of a large capitalization stock or a small capitalization stock. To many portfolio managers, a large capitalization stock will have a capitalization greater than $1 or $2 billion. A small capitalization company will have a market value of less than $1 billion, although some small cap portfolio managers limit their investments to stocks with less than $750 or $500 million in capitalization.

---

the balanced fund, bond fund, or one or more of the specialty funds described in this section.

By themselves, the specialty funds are generally more risky than the "core" funds described previously. Because their investments are in smaller market niches, the specialty funds tend to have greater price fluctuation. Of course, over time you are paid for the higher risk with higher returns.

When used with the core funds, the specialty funds provide not only the benefits of higher returns but also reduce the volatility of the entire portfolio. This concept—diversification—will be discussed in greater detail in Chapter 5.

Small Cap Fund

The small cap fund—short for small capitalization fund—invests in the stocks of smaller companies. These companies tend to be young and in many cases poised for growth. There are numerous examples of small companies that underwent tremendous growth in their early years: Microsoft, MCI, Apple Computer, and The GAP stores. But for all the success stories, there are companies that do not take off. They simply fade away, either to be bought by another company or forced into bankruptcy. Investing in small cap stocks thus entails more risk than investing in well-established, large capitalization stocks.

FIGURE 4–3
Small Capitalization Stocks (Annual Returns 1970–1993)

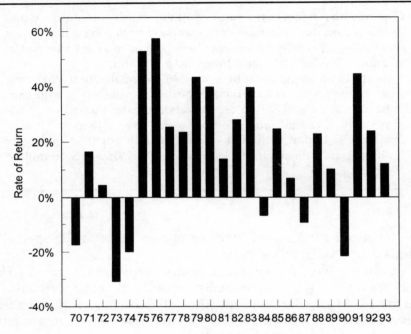

Nevertheless, small capitalization stocks have outperformed the broad market over time, so these funds provide a way to get even greater growth in your equity investment. Small cap funds will probably have more volatility than typical large cap equity funds, but over longer periods they have outperformed large cap stocks. Figure 4–3 compares a small cap stock index with the S&P 500 Index. Since 1970, the best year for small cap stocks was 1976, when the small cap index returned 57.4 percent. The worst year was 1973, when small cap stocks returned –30.9 percent.

Growth Funds

Another popular equity investment vehicle for 401(k) plans is a growth fund. A growth fund emphasizes stocks of companies that have earnings growth rates that are higher than other companies.

TABLE 4–4
*Large Cap Stock Returns versus Small Cap Stock Returns 1926–1993
(66 years)*

	Average Annual Return	*Standard Deviation*
Large Cap	12.3%	20.5%
Small Cap	17.6%	34.8%

Source: Ibbotson Associates

The higher earnings growth rates usually translate into premium stock prices. In many instances, growth companies are better able to weather recessions and their stock market prices remain relatively higher than other stocks. However, when a growth company stumbles, its price can plummet. From time to time, growth stocks, as a group, fall out of favor, usually when they become substantially overvalued relative to the rest of the market. At that point, they may go through long periods of low performance. Like other specialty funds available in your 401(k) plan, growth funds should be used only as a portion of your portfolio.

INTERNATIONAL AND GLOBAL FUNDS

Increasingly popular 401(k) options are global and international funds. These funds invest in companies whose principal activities are outside the United States.

In 1993, the U.S. stock market accounted for approximately 40 percent of the world's larger stock markets. A global stock fund manager will buy stocks in any of the world's markets, while an international stock fund will invest only outside the United States. Figure 4–5 compares returns for the Morgan Stanley EAFE (Europe, Australia, Far East) Index with the S&P 500 Index.

Investing in funds that invest in stocks outside of the United States adds more diversification to your portfolio. The economies of individual countries do not move in lockstep. Frequently, one group of countries will be undergoing a spurt of economic growth, while others will be in a recession. A fund that invests all over the

FIGURE 4–4
International versus U.S. Stocks

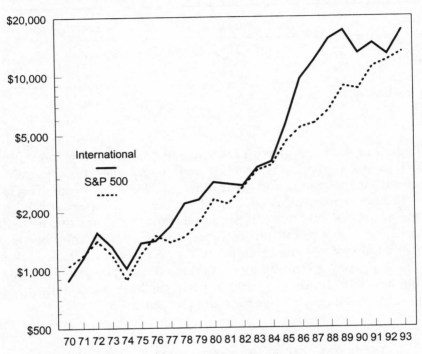

The graph compares the performance of an investment of $1,000 in international stocks with U.S. stocks over a 23-year period. The international investment grew to $12,795 compared with $11,951 for the U.S. investments. Notice, however, that since 1988 the U.S. market has done better than international stocks. This is an example of the volatility that international investors must accept.

world can move from country to country, anticipating economic cycles and avoiding countries with slow economic growth.

Also, the investment manager has more flexibility in selecting stocks. Suppose automobile stocks appear to be attractive because consumers are willing to buy. A fund that invests only in the United States will have to choose between Ford, Chrysler, and General Motors. A fund that invests globally can invest in those three, plus Toyota, Honda, Nissan, Daimler Benz, BMW, and

FIGURE 4–5
International versus U.S. Stocks
Periods Ending 1992

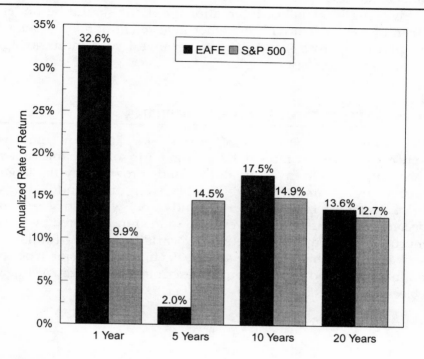

TABLE 4–5
U.S. Stock Returns versus International Stock Returns 1970–1993

	Average Annual Return	Standard Deviation
U.S. Stocks	12.5%	15.8%
Non-U.S. Stocks	14.9%	23.3%

others. The portfolio manager simply has more choices. Global investing also adds a new risk to the investing equation. Investing outside the United States introduces currency risk. Depending on a host of economic and political factors, the value of the U.S. dollar may rise or fall relative to the currencies of other countries. When that happens, it is possible that the value of your investment will change. Stock price gains can diminish significantly during periods when the value of the dollar is rising relative to the currencies of other countries.

Investing in global or international options should be undertaken in conjunction with the other investment options provided by your company's 401(k) plan. Never invest your entire savings in one investment option.

OTHER INVESTMENT OPTIONS

Depending on the structure of your 401(k) plan, your company may offer you many more options. A minority of companies allow their employees to invest in all the funds provided by the larger mutual fund companies like Fidelity, Vanguard, and T. Rowe Price. Having a large number of funds from which to select can become very confusing. However, all of the funds offered by these mutual fund companies are simply variations of the funds described in this chapter. Table 4–6 breaks down the major types of mutual funds and provides broad descriptions of their investment objectives and risk relative to each other.

TABLE 4–6
Types of Mutual Funds Used by 401(k) Plans

Type	Description	Risk Level
Equity Funds		
Aggressive growth	Seeks rapid growth of capital, often through investment in smaller companies and with investment techniques involving greater-than-average risk, such as frequent trading, leveraging, and short selling.	Aggressive
Equity-income	Seeks current income by investing at least 65 percent of its assets in equity securities with above-average yields.	Moderate

TABLE 4–6
Continued

Type	Description	Risk Level
Growth	Seeks capital appreciation by investing primarily in equity securities. Current income, if considered at all, is a secondary objective.	Moderate to aggressive
Growth and income	Seeks growth of capital and current income as near-equal objectives, primarily by investing in equity securities with above-average yields and some potential for appreciation.	Moderate
Foreign stock	Invests primarily in equity securities of issuers located outside of the United States.	Aggressive
World stock	Invests primarily in equity securities of issuers located throughout the world, maintaining a percentage of assets (normally 25% to 50%) in the United States.	Aggressive
Small company	Seeks capital appreciation by investing primarily in stocks of small companies, as determined by market capitalization.	Aggressive
Hybrid Funds		
Asset allocation	Seeks both income and capital appreciation by determining the optimal percentage of assets to place in stocks, bonds, and cash. A top priority of managers of these funds is determining the correct allocation of assets to these sectors, a decision often based on an analysis of business-cycle trends. Sometimes separate managers will handle each class of security, and an allocator will oversee the process of determining the percentage of assets each class receives.	Moderate to aggressive
Balanced	Seeks both income and capital appreciation by investing in a generally fixed combination of both stocks and bonds. In general, these funds will hold a minimum of 25 percent in stocks and 25 percent in bonds at any time.	Moderate

TABLE 4–6
Continued

Type	Description	Risk Level
Income	Invests in both equity and fixed-income securities primarily for the purpose of realizing current income. These funds generally will not invest more than 50 percent of their assets in equities. The percentage of assets in stocks and bonds typically aren't fixed, as they are in balanced funds.	Conservative
Convertible bonds	Invests primarily in bonds and preferred stocks that can be converted into common stocks.	Moderate
Corporate bond high-yield	Seeks income by generally investing 65 percent or more of its assets in bonds rated below investment grade. The price of these issues generally is affected more by the condition of the issuing company (similar to a stock) than by the interest-rate fluctuation that usually causes bond prices to move up and down.	Aggressive
World bond	Seeks current income with capital appreciation as a secondary objective by investing primarily in bonds.	Aggressive
Fixed Income		
Corporate bond—general	Seeks income by investing in fixed-income securities, primarily corporate bonds of various quality ratings.	Moderate
Corporate bond—high quality	Seeks income by investing in fixed-income securities, at least 65 percent of which are rated A or higher.	Conservative to moderate*
Government bond—general	Seeks income by investing in a blend of mortgage-backed securities, Treasuries, and government agencies.	Conservative to moderate*

TABLE 4–6
Concluded

Type	Description	Risk Level
Government bond—mortgage	Seeks income by generally investing at least 65 percent of its assets in securities backed by mortgages, such as securities issued by the Government National Mortgage Association (GNMA), the Federal National Mortgage Association (FNMA), and the Federal Home Loan Mortgage Corporation (FHLMC).	Conservative to moderate*
Government bond—treasury	Seeks income by generally investing at least 80 percent of its assets in U.S. Treasury securities.	Conservative to moderate*
Money market	Seeks income by investing in high quality corporate and U.S. Treasury securities with maturities of one year or less.	Conservative

*Level of risk is determined by the fund's average maturity of its securities. Funds with average maturities of five years or less should be considered conservative investments.

Source for description of funds (other than money market funds): *Morningstar Mutual Fund User's Guide.*

READ THE PROSPECTUS

To fully understand the risk and investment objectives of each fund option, you must read the fund's prospectus. The prospectus can be an intimidating document that is filled with language only a lawyer could love. The critical parts of the prospectus for participants in 401(k) plans are the following sections:

- Investment objectives
- Performance
- Risk
- Fees

When you don't understand parts of the prospectus, ask your benefits representative for an explanation. Also contact the Investment Company Institute (see References) and request their publication, *An Investor's Guide to Reading the Mutual Fund Prospectus*, which provides an easy-to-understand explanation of all parts of the prospectus.

SUMMARY

- The typical 401(k) plan offers several investment options from which to choose. Usually there is a safety of principal fund, an equity fund, and a company stock fund (if the company you work for has publicly traded stock).
- Other core funds include balanced and bond funds.
- Specialty funds include small capitalization, growth, and international or global funds.

Chapter Five

Milestones: Developing and Changing Your Investment Strategies

C hances are that among all the documents your company gave you on the 401(k) plan you will find statements like these:

> The company does not recommend or endorse any particular investment mix. No representations are being made as to the specific performance of any fund. No statement in this brochure should be construed as a recommendation or solicitation to invest in any of the investment options described.

These statements disturb many participants. They should not. With some legal sounding words, your company is recognizing that investing requires a personal decision. All participants in the plan must make their own decisions on the amount to allocate to each investment option. Deciding how to invest your savings is called *asset allocation.*

Making your personal 401(k) plan asset allocation decision requires you to consider the amount of risk that you are willing to take, the number of years before you will need the money, and other sources of savings and retirement income. Your decision should be flexible. You should change your asset allocation as you get older and circumstances in your life change.

DIVERSIFICATION

Diversification, the process of spreading your savings across a range of investments, is an essential part of asset allocation. Diversifying your assets among the different investment options offered by your 401(k) plan can reduce risks while maintaining—or even increasing—your return. It not only opens up your portfolio to additional opportunities, but also decreases the possibility that any single event or development in the stock or bond markets will disrupt your long-range plan.

Figure 5–1 helps you to understand the power of diversification by considering two investments that behave exactly opposite of each other. When the price of investment A goes up, the price of investment B goes down. In addition, if you own either investment, over time you will have identical returns. However, by owning both investments in one portfolio, the ups and downs are eliminated. You obtain the same investment return without price volatility. Of course, it is unlikely that two investments like this exist. However, by investing in a portfolio of different investments, a significant level of diversification will occur. It won't prevent the portfolio from declining in value, but it will smooth out the returns and make them less volatile.

Three Ways to Achieve Diversification

Three types of diversification are available to you as a 401(k) plan investor.

Securities diversification.   Except for the company stock fund option, all of the portfolios in which you invest will have numerous securities. Each security will react differently to events in the market. Thus, if one company enters bankruptcy or reports poor earnings, only a small portion of the portfolio is affected. It is possible that at the same time two companies announce results which will cause the price of one company's securities to decline in value while the other company's will increase.

Portfolio diversification.   By investing in three or more of the investment options offered in your company's 401(k) plan, you can obtain another powerful element of diversification. Stock

FIGURE 5–1
Perfect Diversification

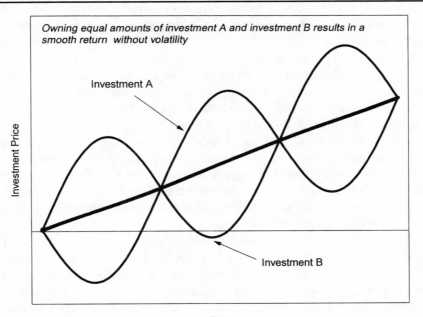

and bond markets do not move up and down in price in the same direction. They react differently to developments in the economy, so it is possible, for example, that the bond market will rally when the stock market is declining. You can take advantage of this if you are investing in both an equity fund and a bond fund.

Types of stocks do not always move in price the same way. Large capitalization stock funds often will behave differently than small capitalization stock funds or growth funds. Price movements of stocks in international or global funds will behave much differently than U.S. stock funds.

If your 401(k) plan provides you with multiple investment options that include an international stock fund and bond fund, a broad slump in the U.S. stock market—and your 401(k) plan's U.S. equity option—can be tempered or, if you are fortunate, offset by gains in bonds or non-U.S. securities.

Diversification through investments outside the 401(k) plan. You can achieve even greater diversification by considering your 401(k) investments with your investments outside the plan. For example, if you own your own home, own other real estate, or have other investments, think about them when setting up your 401(k) plan investment portfolio. For example, it is not a good idea to own only the company stock fund in the 401(k) plan and only company stock in your savings outside the plan. All of your investment assets would be tied to the performance of your company. As discussed in Chapter 4, any one stock can have great price volatility. By investing in only company stock, you create an undiversified portfolio subject to a great deal of price volatility.

However, if you own company stock within the 401(k) plan and invest in bonds or real estate outside the plan, you increase the diversification of your investments and smooth out the price volatility of your long-term investments.

To be sure, the very nature of diversification means that you are less likely to score the really huge gains that a stocks-only portfolio potentially offers. Nor does diversification guarantee that your portfolio will not experience interim declines. But it does increase the likelihood that you will make steady and consistent progress toward your retirement savings goal, with fewer "bumps" along the way.

MAKING ASSET ALLOCATION DECISIONS

Investing in several of the funds offered in your 401(k) plan allows you to tailor a portfolio to your unique needs. The portfolio that you develop should take into consideration your age, your tolerance for risk, and the other financial factors affecting your life. Each year, as you get closer to retirement and your financial situation changes, you should review your asset allocation decision and make any necessary adjustments.

For example, you may want to stay in the same funds you now own but change the proportion of assets allocated to each. Let's say you have most of your savings in the stock funds offered in your company's plan. You might want to gradually move some of your savings to the bond or balanced fund options as you near retirement. The appropriate mix of funds for your

---

Tax Planning with the 401(k) Plan

If you have significant investments outside your 401(k) plan, you may want to consult a tax advisor to help you develop the best investment strategy. Depending on income tax rates and the differences between the rates for ordinary income taxes and capital gains taxes, there are different combinations of portfolios that offer the greatest tax savings while providing you the benefits of diversification and growth.

---

portfolio will depend on two main factors: how long you have to invest and how much risk you are willing to take.

The most important variable is likely to be the number of years remaining until you retire, because the very notion of risk changes over time. Over shorter periods, price fluctuations are your biggest concern. For that reason, if you are near retirement, you will want to be more conservative in your investment selections. Safety of principal is important, but over longer periods the main risk you face is loss of purchasing power to inflation. Therefore, growth of principal is paramount.

In order to stay ahead of inflation, even if you are nearing retirement, it makes sense to keep part of your money in growth-oriented investments like the stock funds that your plan offers. Remember, just because you stop working, inflation doesn't.

When making the asset allocation decision for your 401(k) plan, don't forget your other financial assets: savings account, real estate investments, other mutual fund, or stock or bond investments. For example, Jim has $20,000 in his 401(k) plan and $20,000 in savings accounts. He is conservative but recognizes the need for asset growth to be able to live on his savings in retirement. Jim decides to invest his entire 401(k) plan balance in the stock funds offered by his company's plan and keep the money outside the plan in savings accounts, CDs, and a bond mutual fund. He figures that his retirement savings will get the maximum growth and the savings outside the 401(k) plan will provide a cushion for unexpected expenses. Initially, his allocation is a mix of 50 percent stock and 50 percent cash and bonds.

WHEN TO CHANGE THE ASSET ALLOCATION

Your portfolio will always be changing. Jim was comfortable with a mix of 50 percent stocks and 50 percent bonds and cash. If the stock fund did well and showed considerable gains in the first year of his plan, he might end the year with 60 percent of his assets in the stock fund and 40 percent in bonds and CDs. If Jim chose to stay with his original plan, he might want to reallocate 10 percent of his assets in the 401(k) plan from the stock fund to the bond fund his company offers. By doing so, he would return to his 50 percent stock and 50 percent bond allocation. The reallocation process is called *rebalancing* the portfolio.

Even if all of your financial assets are in your 401(k) plan, rebalancing the portfolio periodically is a good practice. There is no fixed rule when it should be done. Many financial planners suggest that you should rebalance only when your asset allocation becomes distorted by moves in the market. If you had put 20 percent in your 401(k) plan's bond fund, 40 percent in the balanced fund, and 40 percent in the equity fund, and these allocations do not change by more than 10 percent, you probably do not need to rebalance. But when the stock or bond market moves up significantly, and the original allocation changes so that now you have 30 percent bonds, 50 percent balanced, and 20 percent stocks, you may want to rebalance to your original percentages.

The other time you may wish to change your asset allocation is when circumstances change in your life. Reasons for adopting a more conservative asset allocation closer to retirement are discussed later in this chapter.

MARKET TIMING

Probably every investor has dreamed about making a perfect market timing call. Wouldn't it be wonderful if you could invest your money at precisely the moment the stock market reaches the bottom of a cycle, right before the rebound? And then sell your investment at the peak of the market before it declines?

It would be great, but in the real world, market timing is difficult to determine and is therefore a matter of chance. Suppose you

TABLE 5–1
1975–1993 S&P 500

Six Best Performing Months

	Return
Jan. 87	13.41%
Jan. 75	12.73%
Jan. 76	12.17%
Aug. 82	12.13%
Oct. 82	11.51%
Dec. 91	11.43%

Six Worst Performing Months

	Return
Oct. 87	−21.55%
Mar. 80	−9.75%
Aug. 90	−9.03%
Oct. 78	−8.75%
Sept. 86	−8.27%
Nov. 87	−8.18%

invested your money in a fund that achieved the same returns as the S&P 500 Index. If you had invested on January 1, 1975, and never made a withdrawal, your account would have increased by 1,386 percent by December 31, 1993. But if you were market timing and missed the best six months during those 19 years, your total return would have been 644 percent—less than half.

Table 5–1 shows that when the stock market moves, it can jump. If you miss a good month because you are waiting for the perfect time to buy, you can hurt your overall return.

Many 401(k) plans allow you to switch among the investment options every month or even daily. There is a temptation to try to time the markets. Resist it! Few, if any, investment professionals have successfully timed the market over the long run. If they can't do it with their sophisticated research and computer models, there is no reason for you to think you will be any more successful.

HOW TO IMPLEMENT YOUR ASSET ALLOCATION

If frequent shifting of your 401(k) plan investment options is not a good idea, how should you implement large changes in asset allocation? The best approach is to take it slowly. Make your changes gradually.

Lisa, now 35 years old, had been investing in her company's 401(k) plan for 10 years. Because she really didn't understand a great deal about investing, all of her contributions were allocated to the income fund, which is a safety of principal fund. After attending a seminar and reading more about 401(k) plan investing, Lisa decided that a more appropriate mix would be 50 percent in the equity fund, 10 percent in the small capitalization stock fund, 20 percent in the balanced fund, and 20 percent in the income fund. She had accumulated $15,000 in her account, and the company's plan allowed her to shift funds among the various investment options once a month. Since Lisa's company required the shifts to be made in increments of no less than 10 percent, she developed a plan to take three months to move her assets.

Fund	January	February	March	April
Income	100%	60%	30%	20%
Balanced		30%	30%	20%
Equity		10%	30%	50%
Small cap equity			10%	10%
Total	100%	100%	100%	100%

Each month Lisa instructed her benefits representative to shift the assets among the various funds to achieve the desired long-term asset allocation.

The reason for moving gradually is to avoid sudden downturns in the markets (see Table 5–1). You don't want to get caught in a month that has a decline in value. By moving your allocation gradually, you avoid putting all your assets into a fund at the same time the market declines. Like many of the strategies discussed in this book, it helps minimize volatility.

	Agree	Disagree
What Type of 401(k) Plan Investor Are You?		
1. I am comfortable with the idea that when I invest in stocks and bonds the value of my portfolio can move down in value over some periods of time.	___	___
2. I believe that over time stocks will outperform more conservative investments.	___	___
3. In my 401(k) plan, I plan to take the long-term view and save for retirement.	___	___
4. I have savings outside the 401(k) plan to cover large expenses such as a home purchase or college tuition.	___	___
5. My job is secure, or if I found myself having to change jobs, I could do so without using my 401(k) savings to pay expenses between jobs.	___	___
6. I think I can take more risk in my 401(k) plan because my company also provides a pension plan that will provide part of my retirement income.	___	___
7. If I left my current employer, I would invest the proceeds from the 401(k) plan in my new company's 401(k) plan or an IRA.	___	___

If the plan allows you to move assets from fund to fund less frequently than once a month, you need to adjust your schedule to fit your plan's rules. For example, if your plan allows only two shifts a year, you might make an initial shift and wait three or four months to shift the remainder of your assets into the new asset allocation arrangement.

ASSET ALLOCATION STRATEGIES

While you are the only one who can decide on the best asset allocation strategy for you, Tables 5–2 to 5–5 serve as a guide to help you in setting your asset mix. The tables address the funds typically found in a 401(k) plan. The possible funds are divided into three categories: conservative, moderate, and aggressive. Within each category are two or three representative funds. If your plan offers more options, place them in the category you believe is appropriate.

The distinction between conservative, moderate, and aggressive lies in the amount of volatility versus the return expected in each fund. With a conservative fund, you should expect safety of principal, little volatility, and modest returns. At the other end of the spectrum, the aggressive funds will have wide price fluctuations and the highest expected returns.

To use the tables effectively, you need to identify the type of investor you are. Again, there are three categories: conservative, moderate, and aggressive. Before placing yourself in one of these categories, think about the questions in the box on page 67 titled, "What Type of 401(k) Plan Investor Are You?"

These statements are designed to make you think about your approach to risk.

Conservative Investors

If you disagree with these statements, you probably are a conservative investor or need to seek stability because of financial circumstances. Your financial circumstances dictate that you should invest in the conservative and moderate risk investment choices offered by your 401(k) plans. These include the safety of principal fund, short-term and intermediate bond funds, and the balanced fund.

Moderate Investors

If you agree with some, but not all, of the statements, you probably are in a position to take a moderate amount of risk in your investing. The majority of 401(k) investors can probably take a moderate level of risk. Investors in this category are relying wholly on their 401(k) plan for retirement savings, but they also may have to dip into those savings if emergencies arise. A diversified 401(k) portfolio of stock, bond, and safety of principal funds should meet the needs of the investor who can take a moderate level of risk.

Aggressive Investors

If you found yourself agreeing with most of the statements, consider yourself an aggressive investor. This doesn't classify you as a daredevil! It means that you have the assets outside the plan and the job stability to invest in equities in the 401(k) plan. This investment will provide you with the highest expected return and the greatest volatility. However, since you have the financial strength and a long-term view of investing, you should be able to weather any downturn in the markets easily.

SAMPLE ASSET ALLOCATION STRATEGIES

Let's look at how the amount of risk you are willing to take translates into an investment portfolio. Remember, these are sample portfolios designed to help you think about the best asset allocation for you.

The 20s and 30s: The Golden Years of Investing

The golden years of investing occur when you are in your 20s and 30s. Investments you make during those years can take maximum advantage of the power of compounding. Table 2–2 shows what happens when you save even small amounts and let it grow for 30 years or more. Although you will have many bills at this time of your life and your salary may not be as high as you would like it to be, make every effort to put away some money in your 401(k) plan. This is doubly true if your company provides a matching contribution. The matching contribution means your company is helping you save. Take advantage of it!

Even the conservative investor at this age can afford to put some savings into equity investments. The exception might be if you plan to make an early withdrawal from the plan. If that's the case, you should set up an allocation that looks more like that of someone five years away from retirement. Before you start depending on an early withdrawal, see Chapter 7 for the penalties and how much you will be giving up.

TABLE 5–2
30 Years Old, 35 Years to Retirement

	Type of Investor		
Type of Fund	*Conservative: Low Market Risk* *High Inflation Risk*	*Moderate: Moderate Market Risk* *Moderate Inflation Risk*	*Aggressive: High Market Risk* *Low Inflation Risk*
Conservative			
Safety of principal fund	20%	10%	0%
Intermediate maturity bond	10%	0%	0%
Moderate			
Balanced fund (½ equity)	20%	30%	20%
Equity fund	30%	30%	20%
Aggressive			
Growth or small cap fund	10%	10%	20%
International or global	0%	10%	20%
Company stock fund	10%	10%	20%
Total	100%	100%	100%
Equity exposure	60%	75%	90%

The 40s: Full Steam Ahead

In your 40s, you hope to reach a point where the growth in your spending has slowed down. During these years, you should maximize your savings in the 401(k) plan. Every dollar that you can afford to save now will have 15 to 25 years to grow. There is plenty of time to let the capital appreciation of your plan's equity fund help your retirement savings balance grow.

Don't forget to save outside the 401(k) plan for special circumstances like college tuition, home repair, and financial emergencies. That way you can leave your 401(k) savings untouched until retirement.

TABLE 5–3
40 Years Old, 25 Years to Retirement

	Type of Investor		
	Conservative: Low Market Risk	*Moderate: Moderate Market Risk*	*Aggressive: High Market Risk*
Type of Fund	*High Inflation Risk*	*Moderate Inflation Risk*	*Low Inflation Risk*
Conservative			
Safety of principal fund	20%	10%	0%
Intermediate maturity bond	30%	20%	10%
Moderate			
Balanced fund (½ equity)	20%	10%	10%
Equity fund	10%	20%	20%
Aggressive			
Growth or small cap fund	10%	15%	20%
International or global	0%	15%	20%
Company stock fund	10%	10%	20%
Total	100%	100%	100%
Equity exposure	40%	65%	85%

The 50s: Start Now to Develop Retirement Strategies

Although compounding still has time to work, a particularly tough bear market could dampen your overall return when you are in your 50s, with 15 years left to the usual retirement age. As you grow closer to 60 years old, gradually reduce your equity exposure. There is an underlying assumption within the figures shown in Table 5–4 that the aggressive investor has adequate funds outside the 401(k) plan to absorb any long-term stock market downturns. In addition, the aggressive investor, with a 70 percent stock allocation, may be planning to work past age 65.

TABLE 5–4
50 Years Old, 15 Years to Retirement

	Type of Investor		
	Conservative: Low Market Risk	Moderate: Moderate Market Risk	Aggressive: High Market Risk
Type of Fund	High Inflation Risk	Moderate Inflation Risk	Low Inflation Risk
Conservative			
Safety of principal fund	20%	20%	0%
Intermediate maturity bond	30%	20%	20%
Moderate			
Balanced fund (½ equity)	30%	20%	20%
Equity fund	20%	20%	20%
Aggressive			
Growth or small cap fund	0%	0%	10%
International or global	0%	10%	20%
Company stock fund	0%	10%	10%
Total	100%	100%	100%
Equity exposure	35%	50%	70%

During your 50s, you should contact your company's benefits representative to learn the details of how retirement works in your company. See Chapter 8 for details on retirement planning.

The 60s: The Home Stretch

Within five years of retirement, you should cut back on equities to provide liquidity. At retirement, a rule of thumb is to have five years of income in a stable safety of principal fund. To the extent that you have savings above what you need for the first five years of retirement, you should continue to invest in equities. If you are healthy at age 65, you can expect 20 years or more of retirement. During those retirement years, inflation will continue to be a risk that you have to beat.

TABLE 5–5
60 Years Old, 5 Years to Retirement

Type of Fund	Conservative: Low Market Risk / High Inflation Risk	Moderate: Moderate Market Risk / Moderate Inflation Risk	Aggressive: High Market Risk / Low Inflation Risk
Conservative			
Safety of principal fund	20%	20%	10%
Intermediate maturity bond	50%	15%	20%
Moderate			
Balanced fund (½ equity)	20%	30%	20%
Equity fund	10%	25%	30%
Aggressive			
Growth or small cap fund	0%	0%	10%
International or global	0%	10%	10%
Company stock fund	0%	0%	0%
Total	100%	100%	100%
Equity exposure	20%	50%	60%

When You Can't Sell Shares in the Company Stock Fund

There is no right or wrong answer about the allocation of your investments. The tables assume that you have control over the amount of company stock in your portfolio. If your company provides a matching contribution in shares of company stock and does not let you *sell the shares,* adjust the overall equity exposure in each scenario to compensate for the allocation to the company stock fund. For the moderate and aggressive investors, there should still be some small cap, aggressive growth, and international exposure in your portfolio, even if a large part of your portfolio must be held in company stock.

SUMMARY

- Spreading your assets among several funds— diversification—helps smooth investment returns over the long run.
- Each year, you should review your asset allocation and rebalance the fund choices to maintain your investment objectives.
- Trying to determine the perfect time to enter or exit markets is risky. Even the professional money managers have a poor track record on market timing.
- Move assets in and out of your plan's investment funds over a period of months to achieve the benefits of averaging.
- Consider all your financial assets when making 401(k) plan investment decisions.

Chapter Six

How Well Is My Investment Doing?

O nce you have begun to make your investment in the 401(k) plan, you will want to know how you are doing. Is your nest egg growing the way you expected? That should be easy to find out. Right? All you have to do is read your 401(k) plan valuation statement and see if the amount you put into the plan has gone up in value.

Bill keeps all of his plan's valuation statements. Each quarter he checks whether the value of each of his three investment funds has gone up. They always have. He assumes his performance has been pretty good.

What is wrong with the way Bill is looking at his statements? Bill contributes with each paycheck, and his company matches his contribution. Because of these contributions, the value of his account is always rising. Bill really does not know how well his investment options are performing.

To measure the performance of each of your funds, you must calculate the results after *subtracting* the contributions, withdrawals, and reallocations between funds. You must answer the question, "How would I have done if there had been no deposits or withdrawals in my account throughout the period?"

Table 6–1 contains some information from Bill's latest quarterly valuation statement.

TABLE 6–1
Bill's Fund Choices

	Safety of Principal	Equity	Company Stock	Total
Beginning balance	$10,000.00	$5,000.00	$5,000.00	$20,000.00
Investment return	181.00	250.00	–60.00	371.00
Contributions	225.00	225.00	225.00	675.00
Withdrawals	0.00	0.00	0.00	0.00
Ending balance	$10,406.00	$5,475.00	$5,165.00	$21,046.00

All of Bill's funds had a higher balance at the end than at the beginning of the period; he saw his total savings rise from $20,000 to $21,046 in the quarter—a 5.2 percent increase. However, more than half of that increase came from Bill's contributions. His investments increased by $371, or about 1.9 percent. In this particular quarter, Bill made money in the safety of principal and equity funds, but lost money in his company stock fund.

What does a 1.9 percent increase mean? Was Bill's investment return respectable?

ABSOLUTE RETURN

You should look at investment performance in two ways: on an absolute basis and on a relative basis. Let's first see how Bill would decide whether his absolute return was OK.

Absolute return should be measured against your investment goals.

Let's assume that Bill's starting balance represented the asset allocation with which he was most comfortable. He had 50 percent of his assets in the safety of principal fund and 50 percent of his assets in equity—25 percent in the equity fund and 25 percent in the company stock fund. Over the long term, Bill expects his equity investments to achieve a rate of return 6 percent above inflation.

TABLE 6–2
Bill's Total Returns

Fund	Annual Expected Return	Allocation to the Fund	Return Contribution
Safety of principal	5%	50%	2.5%
Equity fund	10%	25%	2.5%
Company stock fund	10%	25%	2.5%
Total expected return			7.5%

Thus, if inflation is 4 percent, Bill expects to achieve a 10 percent average annual rate of return. He expects the safety of principal fund to achieve a rate of return equal to inflation plus 1 percent, or about 5 percent a year when the annual rate of inflation is 4 percent. Table 6–2 shows how each fund will contribute to the total expected return of Bill's asset allocation.

On an absolute basis, Bill will have done well each year that the return on his investment choices exceeds 7.5 percent. His investments will have underperformed his expectations each year that they return less than 7.5 percent. It is important to remember that the evaluation of absolute returns must be made over several years. The markets are volatile; you should expect to have some superior years, some average years, and some poor years. What counts is reaching your expected average return over a number of years.

To return to Bill's single quarterly return of 1.9 percent. Was it OK? Realizing that one quarter is a very short period of measurement, Bill could think about his 1.9 percent return this way: If he achieved four quarters in a row of 1.9 percent, his one-year compounded return would be 7.8 percent. For his particular asset allocation, he expects an annual rate of return of 7.5 percent. Therefore, his quarterly return of 1.9 was slightly above his expectations. However, given the volatility of equity markets, 1.9 percent is neither good nor bad. A 1.9 percent quarterly return is well within the range of likely possibilities, so the return for Bill's portfolio should be considered satisfactory.

TABLE 6–3
Typical Fund Benchmarks

Type of Fund	Typical Benchmarks
Safety of principal funds	Consumer Price Index 90-day Treasury bills Merrill Lynch 1–3 year Treasuries
Bond fund	Lehman Bros. Govt./Corp. Index Salomon Bros. Broad Index
U.S. equity funds	S&P 500 Wilshire 5000
U.S. growth	S&P 500 Wilshire 5000
U.S. small cap	Russell 2000 S&P Mid-Cap
International fund	Morgan Stanley Capital International EAFE Index
Global fund	Morgan Stanley Capital International World Index

RELATIVE RETURN

Relative returns compare each individual fund's return with other funds that have a similar investment goal. This is called comparing a fund to a *benchmark*. Table 6–3 lists benchmarks typically used in various kinds of funds.

Let's look at Bill's equity fund option, which had a 5 percent return in the quarter. The company's investment materials explain the investment objectives of this fund: It will be actively managed and invested in large capitalization stocks of companies based in the United States. A reasonable benchmark for this fund is Standard & Poor's (S&P) 500 Index, an index of 500 of the largest U.S. stocks by market capitalization (see Chapter 4 for an explanation of indexes).

If the S&P 500 returned 4.5 percent in this particular quarter, on a relative basis Bill's equity fund would have done well. It beat a passively managed fund that invested in all 500 stocks in the index. If the S&P 500 had done 5.5 percent, Bill's equity fund would have underperformed the index.

TABLE 6–4
Equity Fund

	Account Size	Annual Return	Total Cumulative Return	Annualized Rate of Return	Theoretical Ending Balance*
Starting Balance	$10,000				
End of Year 1	$11,000	10%	10%	10.2%	$11,016
End of Year 2	$10,450	–5%	5%	10.2%	$12,135
End of Year 3	$13,063	25%	31%	10.2%	$13,368
End of Year 4	$14,108	8%	41%	10.2%	$14,726
End of Year 5	$16,224	15%	62%	10.2%	$16,224

* The theoretical ending balance shows what the ending balance of the account would have been if it had achieved the annualized rate of return each year.

When measuring relative return, you are making a comparison relative only to its benchmark. For example, suppose the annual return for the S&P 500 is –10 percent and that of the equity fund provided by your company only –8 percent. On a relative basis, you did very well! On an absolute basis, you have lost ground against your long-term investment objectives and have not done well.

ANNUALIZED RETURN

Frequently, investment managers and fund brochures will present returns on an annualized basis. Annualizing returns removes the volatility from individual years. It is similar to averaging returns, but it takes into account the compounded growth of the assets. The example (see Table 6–4) assumes that you make no contributions and no withdrawals from an equity fund.

This account started with $10,000. At the end of five years, the account balance was $16,224. Because the account was invested in stocks, the returns were volatile. After a good start in year 1, the account lost money in year 2. Years 3, 4, and 5 experienced positive returns. The account's total return over the five years was up 62 percent.

The account also would have gained 62 percent if the return in each year was 10.16 percent (10.2 percent when rounded). In other words, the annualized return for this account was 10.2 percent. For volatile accounts that show large positive or negative returns in any given year, it helps to review the annualized return to see whether the account's return meets long-term investment objectives.

IS PAST PERFORMANCE THE ONLY CRITERIA?

There is a caveat in most 401(k) brochures, mutual fund prospectuses, and investment-related advertisements: *Past performance is no guarantee of future results.* Even though your equity fund had an annualized return of 10 percent over the last five years, that is no reason to believe it will do so for the next five years. Many factors—the economy, the rate of inflation, interest rates, and investor perceptions—will strongly affect how well your fund performs.

The caveat shown in your 401(k) investment brochure is written by your company's legal department and approved by the U.S. Securities and Exchange Commission. It is designed to make investors aware of the volatility of investing. Once you realize that all investments can be volatile and returns will differ from year to year, the performance record can tell you quite a lot. Let's next discuss one way to analyze the record for an individual fund.

Fund Stability

Obtain the fund's return for each of the last 10 years, and the annual returns for the benchmark used to evaluate the fund. We can use as an example the Investment Company of America (ICA), a $15 billion growth and income mutual fund used in many 401(k) plans (see Table 6–5).

First, look at the difference between the absolute returns each year. The worst year for ICA was 0.7 percent and the best year was 33.0 percent. This happens to be an exceptional 10-year period for stocks. In 1974, this fund had a decline of 17.9 percent while the S&P 500 Index declined by 26.6 percent. While ICA provided its investors with some protection in bear markets, it was not im-

TABLE 6-5
Comparing a Fund to Its Benchmark

Year	Investment Company of America	S&P 500 Index	Annual Difference
1993	11.6%	10.0%	1.6%
1992	7.0%	7.7%	-0.7%
1991	26.5%	30.6%	-4.0%
1990	0.7%	-3.2%	3.9%
1989	29.4%	31.5%	-2.1%
1988	13.3%	16.8%	-3.5%
1987	5.2%	5.2%	0.0%
1986	21.7%	18.4%	3.3%
1985	33.0%	31.9%	1.1%
1984	6.8%	6.2%	0.6%

mune to them. Are you prepared for this level of volatility in your equity fund? (Remember, you are investing for retirement, which may be a number of years away.)

Next, look at the relative performance, the difference between the fund's return and the benchmark. While it is unlikely that an actively managed fund will beat the benchmark in every year, it probably should do better in half of the years. How close is the fund to the benchmark in most years? It also is important to look at years when the market didn't perform well. Did the fund protect its investors from down markets? It is not unusual for an actively managed fund to lag a benchmark in very strong years. On the other hand, you should not expect an actively managed fund to be down as much in years of market declines. In 1992, when the market declined by 3.2 percent, ICA managed a 0.7 percent gain—a good sign.

This analysis also applies to bond funds, safety of principal funds, and growth funds. In making this kind of analysis, it is critical that you compare the results to the appropriate benchmark. For example, growth funds may be compared to the S&P 500 Index, but a more precise measure is to compare them to a group of growth funds that are managed with the same investment objectives. If your growth fund did poorly compared with

---

Value Styles versus Growth Styles

Even within large capitalization funds, the style the portfolio manager uses to make investments will affect the performance of the fund. With a value approach, the portfolio manager will look for stocks that are undervalued by the market. Eventually other investors realize that these stocks are undervalued and buy them. When this happens value stock prices rise faster than the market average.

The portfolio manager who uses a growth style invests only in companies that have a history and continuing prospect for rapid earnings growth. To investors, these stocks may appear to be overvalued compared with other stocks, but the growth portfolio manager believes that the growth rates will continue into the future and the stock prices will rise faster than the market average.

---

the S&P 500 Index but did better than all the growth funds with similar investment objectives, then your relative results would appear to be acceptable.

Will This Type of Investment Performance Continue?

There are usually two reasons for an actively managed fund to outperform the broad market benchmarks. The first reason is the investment style of the fund. Among equity funds, various investment styles may be employed. Over shorter periods of time, usually from one to three years, one type of style may be in favor with investors while another is out of favor. The two more common styles are *value* and *growth*. When a style is in favor, all funds of that type will have a tendency to outperform funds that employ another investment style.

The fund's portfolio manager or managers is the second reason a fund will outperform the benchmark. The managers of the fund are doing a good job of buying securities with great potential and selling securities with less potential. When looking at the historical performance of the fund, it is important to make sure that it was achieved by the current manager or managers of the fund.

This is a particular problem for funds that are run by so-called *star managers*; that is, one person who has made all the fund's buy-and-sell decisions. If the star manager leaves the fund, the past record may not indicate the type of performance to expect in the future. If your fund is managed by a committee, a system of multiple portfolio managers, or computerized security selection, then one individual leaving the fund will have less impact.

What if My 401(k) Plan Uses Index Funds?

If your company's 401(k) plan uses index funds instead of actively managed funds, it does not matter who the portfolio manager is. In passively managed index funds, computer-based quantitative techniques try to match the return of the index. You can expect to achieve the return of the index (less any fees) and experience the same volatility.

For example, if your 401(k) plan uses an S&P 500 Index fund for its diversified equity option, the fund will own all 500 stocks, and in the same proportion, as the index. You can expect the same performance and volatility as the index. See Chapter 4 for a more complete description of index funds.

SOURCES OF PERFORMANCE AND FUND INFORMATION

Many 401(k) plans publish newsletters that provide regular updates on how the funds within the plan are performing. When reviewing these materials, check the benchmark for the fund. If the materials do not include a benchmark, ask your benefits representative what it is. Find out whether your company has the information that would allow you to evaluate the fund's performance.

If your fund invests your savings in a mutual fund, there are many other sources of information. The daily newspaper and *The Wall Street Journal* publish the closing price of the fund on the

TABLE 6–6
Wall Street Journal Mutual Fund Reporting

Day of Week	Rate of Return Information Reported (Lipper Analytical Data)
Monday	Year-to-date return and total expense ratio
Tuesday	Year-to-date, 4 weeks, and one year returns
Wednesday	Year-to-date, 13 weeks, and three year* returns
Thursday	Year-to-date, 26 weeks, and four year* returns
Friday	Year-to-date, 39 weeks, and five year* returns

*Annualized

previous business day. In addition, each day of the week *The Wall Street Journal* provides historical returns over different periods (see Table 6–6).

Barron's, Money, Worth, Kiplinger's Personal Finance, Business Week, Fortune, Forbes, and many other business-oriented magazines publish articles on mutual funds. Most provide a quarterly review of performance for the larger mutual funds. You don't have to subscribe to these publications; they should be available at your local library.

Your library also may subscribe to publications by Morningstar, which tracks the performance of more than 2,700 mutual funds and reports on them monthly. Your library may even subscribe to an on-line service that allows you to review the performance of funds by way of a computer database. Your company's corporate finance department or benefits department may have literature that you could copy about the mutual funds in your 401(k) plan.

Finally, the mutual fund companies themselves are a wealth of information. Call or write them directly for annual reports and prospectuses, if your benefits representative can not supply them to you (see Table 6–7).

The more you know about how the funds in your 401(k) plan are managed, the more comfortable you should feel when markets are volatile and prices fluctuate.

TABLE 6–7
Largest 15 Mutual Fund Families Client Service Telephone Numbers

Fidelity Group	800-544-8888
Vanguard Group	800-662-7442
American Funds	800-421-1080
Franklin Group of Funds	800-342-5236
Putnam Mutual Funds	800-225-1581
Merrill Lynch Group	609-282-2800
Dean Witter Funds	800-869-3863
IDS Group	800-328-8300
Dreyfus Group	800-373-9387
T. Rowe Price Funds	800-541-8832
Prudential Mutual Funds	800-225-1852
Kemper Funds	800-621-1048
Twentieth Century Investors Group	800-345-2021
Shearson Group	212-720-9218
Scudder Funds	800-535-2726

WHO PAYS FOR THE FUND?

Operating a 401(k) plan is expensive. When your company established the plan, it had to program new systems to ensure that the money from your paycheck was sent to the trustee to be invested. A trustee is required for a qualified retirement plan such as a 401(k) plan, and most plans use a bank to provide the service. It is the trustee's responsibility to make sure the funds are properly invested and that all of the laws and regulations governing the plan are followed. The trustee will also hold the plan's securities in a vault or through a computer-based investment custody system. Your 401(k) plan literature should disclose the name of the organization that serves as the trustee. The trustee charges your company or the 401(k) plan a fee for this service.

The company also purchased record-keeping software or hired a firm to be the record keeper. (Sometimes the trustee will also serve as the record keeper.) The record keeper makes sure that all contributions and gains and losses from investments are properly credited to your account. The record keeper also keeps track of outstanding loans that may be allowed in your 401(k) plans.

In addition, the salaries of company employees who work on the plan are an expense of the 401(k) plan.

The mutual fund charges a fee for its investment management service. If your company's 401(k) plan has hired an investment management firm to manage a separate account, the firm charges fees for this service. The portfolio manager needs a staff to administer the fund, undertake research, and trade the securities in the portfolio. The firm that actually manages the fund also has to pay salaries and tries to make a profit.

All of the 401(k) plan fees must be paid by either your company or the participants.

If your company uses mutual funds in its 401(k) plan, the investment management fees and other expenses are deducted from the assets in the fund. Mutual funds charge a range of fees from 0.2 percent to about 2.0 percent of the assets under management. The average charges are 1.35 percent for diversified stock mutual funds, 0.95 percent for bond funds, and 0.69 percent for money market funds. These percentages, which indicate the amount of expense divided by the assets under management, are called the expense ratio of the fund.

These fees can have a significant impact. If your fund charges a 1 percent annual fee and your return last year was 4 percent, you "lost" 20 percent of your return in the fee. If the fee had been only 0.5 percent, your return would have been 4.5 percent.

Fees are charged whether the fund does well or not. In a year when the return is 20 percent, a 1 percent fee does not seem like much. But when the markets are lackluster and stocks return 1 percent for the year and your fund charges a 1 percent fee, you have had no investment gain in that year. If your company invests the 401(k) plan funds in a separate account, the company may be paying the investment management fees or it may be passing them on to you by reducing your savings.

The prospectus and materials provided by your company should clearly spell out whether the participants or the company are paying the fees to run the fund. There is no clear trend on who pays the fees. Many companies feel that since they are matching the contributions of the employees, which is a sizable expense, the employees should pay the fees for administering and investing the assets of the fund.

How Much Is Too Much?

Here are some guidelines on fees for 401(k) plans:

- **Load charges.** If your fund is using mutual funds, there should be no load charges. Load charges are paid by individual investors in mutual funds to pay a commission to the broker selling the fund. Because most 401(k) plans are considered institutional investors and do not require the services of a stockbroker, the load charge is waived by the mutual fund companies.

- **Expense ratio.** The expense ratio for the mutual fund or separately managed account should be no more than 1.5 percent of assets for large capitalization diversified equity funds and 1.0 percent for bond funds. Small capitalization equity funds, international funds, global funds, and specialty funds may charge fees that are 1.5–2.0 percent of assets. Look in the prospectus of a mutual fund for the table that shows annual operating expenses as a percent of average net assets. This table will include expense information for management fees, 12b-1 fees (a marketing fee charged by some funds), and other expenses. Most important, it should indicate the total operating expense. This is your guide to how expensive it is to invest in the mutual fund and how much you are paying through your 401(k) plan investments.

- **Administrative expense ratio.** Expenses for the record keeper and trustee will depend on the number of participants in the 401(k) plan. Plans with 100 employees or less might have a fee as high as $100 per participant each year. Funds with more than 5,000 participants should have fees of no more than $20 to $30 per participant.

The exception to these guidelines occurs where the company uses a "bundled" approach for the administration and investment of the 401(k) plan assets. In this case, one firm provides the record keeping, acts as trustee and custodian of the assets, and performs the investment management function. This may make it easier for your company to operate the plan, but it makes keeping track of costs more difficult. It is not unusual for some bundled suppliers to charge lower fees for the record keeping and trust operations, and higher fees for the investment management services. However, the total fees for the entire plan should be the same or less than those of a plan where the company has hired a different supplier for record keeping, trust and custody, and investment management of the plan's funds.

Ask Questions

If the information provided by your company's benefits department seems to be out of line with these guidelines, ask why the fees are so high. Has the fund administrator done any cost comparison studies with other 401(k) plans? Are there special circumstances at the company that warrant higher fees? (Highly diversified companies with many small subsidiaries and different payroll systems generally have higher fees.) Let the benefits department know that minimizing fees is important to you and that you want the most efficient structure for the 401(k) plan.

SUMMARY

- Measure performance by ignoring contributions and withdrawals.
- Absolute return shows how well you are achieving your long-term investment goals.
- Relative return shows how well your investment is performing compared with benchmarks and other funds that have similar investment objectives.

- Annualized rates of return provide a way to look at average returns over several years and eliminate the volatility. It is a common and convenient way to compare the returns of funds over time.

- To analyze the suitability of an investment fund for you, review at least 10 individual years of fund returns. Find out if the same individual or team of individuals managed the fund over the entire period.

- Take into consideration the fees charged by the 401(k) plan, especially if your company is charging all the fees to the plan. Are you getting a good value for the fees charged?

Chapter Seven

Whose Money Is It Anyway?

T he 401(k) plan is an excellent way to set aside money for retirement that will compound tax free and reduce your current
tax bill. However, a 401(k) plan is not the same as a bank savings
account. You cannot call your benefits representative and withdraw money whenever you like.

Robert, now 35 years old, had been saving in the 401(k) plan
since he was 25 years old. His total balance in the plan exceeds
$30,000. He had heard that when he was ready to purchase a new
home, he could withdraw part of his savings to help make the
down payment. However, Robert was surprised that he would
need to withdraw nearly $20,000 and pay the difference in taxes in
order to net $10,000 for the down payment. In addition, he had to
fill out several complicated forms and provide his company with
information about not only his finances but those of his wife and
all other sources of savings. He protested that it was none of the
company's business, but the human resources benefit representative told Robert that because he was taking a hardship withdrawal, the IRS required that all this information be reported and
submitted to a committee for approval.

As an alternative to withdrawing the money from the 401(k)
plan, the benefit representative suggested that Robert consider
taking a loan against his balance. Under his company's loan program, Robert could borrow up to half of his balance—up to a maximum of $50,000—for any purpose and take five years to pay it
back. In addition, because Robert planned to purchase a home
with the proceeds, the plan allowed the term of the loan to be 10
years instead of the usual five.

THE PLAN IS REGULATED BY THE IRS

The 401(k) plan has many rules. The name of these plans—
401(k)—comes from the section of the U.S. Internal Revenue Service Tax Code that allows you and your company to defer taxes.
As any taxpayer knows, the IRS is zealous about collecting taxes.
Therefore, when a vehicle exists to defer taxes, as a 401(k) plan
does, the IRS provides strict regulations that must be followed to
obtain the tax benefit. Three regulations have the most effect on
employees saving in a 401(k) plan: contribution limits, nondiscrimination testing, and early withdrawals.

Contribution Limits

The IRS sets limits on the amount of taxes that can be deferred in a
401(k) plan. These rules limit how much you can save in a 401(k)
plan each year. In 1994, the limit was just over $9,000. Each year,
the limit has been raised at the rate of inflation according to the
Consumer Price Index.

   Another rule requires that your contributions and those made
by your employer (including contributions to any other retirement
plans offered by the company) cannot be greater than 25 percent
of your taxable income, or $30,000, whichever is less. (The $30,000
figure is indexed for inflation.) Under this rule, if you make
$25,000 per year, your limit is $6,250. The rule usually affects only
couples who have two sources of income. If you live on one
spouse's salary and try to maximize the other spouse's savings,
you might bump up against this limit.

Nondiscrimination Tests

Other rules make sure that the plan does not discriminate. The IRS
is not concerned with race or sex discrimination in 401(k) plans. It
wants to prevent companies from favoring higher paid employees
over lower paid employees. The nondiscrimination tests are complicated calculations that your company must make every year to
ensure that the plan does not benefit only a select group of higher
paid employees. In order to meet these regulatory requirements,

some companies have to limit the amount that highly compensated employees can contribute to a 401(k) plan.

If your company has problems passing the IRS nondiscrimination tests and you are one of the highly compensated participants—in 1994, under most circumstances, you would have to earn more than $66,000 a year—then your company will notify you that it has to limit the amount you can contribute to the plan.

Since nondiscrimination testing takes place after the plan year ends, companies sometimes find they have failed the nondiscrimination testing rules after all the payroll deductions have been made. When this happens, highly compensated employees get a portion of their annual contribution refunded. They then have to pay taxes on this portion as if it were ordinary income.

Failure to pass the nondiscrimination test usually happens when the number of lower paid employees participating in the 401(k) plan changes. For example, if the number of lower paid employees who leave the plan is larger than the number of higher paid employees who remain in the plan, the 401(k) plan may no longer pass the nondiscrimination tests.

If you belong to the highly compensated group, you may want to have your benefits representative find out whether your company might have a problem satisfying the nondiscrimination rules. If there is a problem, you should delay filing your income tax returns. If you have already filed your income tax returns, you would have to file an amended return and pay the extra taxes.

WITHDRAWING YOUR SAVINGS BEFORE AGE 59½

The toughest rules for 401(k) plan participants are those concerning withdrawals. It is not easy to get your money out of the plan before you retire or leave the company. The IRS has set 59 1/2 as the age of retirement. After age 59 1/2, your withdrawals will be charged only federal and, if applicable, state and local income taxes.

Generally, withdrawals before age 59 1/2 are more difficult than after that age. They usually require you to pay a penalty tax. However, there are a few exceptions to the age 59 1/2 rule. One occurs if

you take early retirement—or are terminated and choose to retire—at age 55 or older. Distributions after you retire at age 55 are
not charged the 10 percent penalty tax. Other exceptions cover installment payments, medical expenses, disability, and death. Your
employee benefits department can help you determine whether a
withdrawal meets the requirements of one of these exceptions.

In-Service Withdrawals

To maintain the tax-deferred status of the plan for all participants,
your company must tightly control withdrawals while you are
still employed by the company. These are called *in-service withdrawals.* The IRS has established four conditions that permit an in-
service withdrawal without jeopardizing your company's 401(k)
plan's tax-deferred status:

1. When the participant, his or her spouse, or dependents of
   the participant need to pay medical expenses.
2. For costs directly related to the purchase, excluding
   mortgage payments, of a principal residence for the
   employee.
3. For payment of college tuition and related educational fees
   for the next 12 months for the employee, spouse, or
   dependents.
4. To avoid eviction of the employee from his or her principal
   residence or to avoid foreclosure on the mortgage of the
   employee's principal residence.

The circumstance under which you can make an in-service
withdrawal is called the plan's hardship withdrawal provision.
Your company can add to the list of situations where it will allow
a withdrawal, but the IRS requires that the company and the employee show considerable financial need that cannot be met by
any of the employee's other assets.

In most cases, your company will require you to present documents and a financial statement that prove that you have no other
savings and need to make a hardship withdrawal. For example,
you may have to show that you do not have other savings that
could be used to purchase a home, and you must have a contract
to purchase the home.

Early Withdrawal Penalty

After you meet the requirements for a hardship withdrawal, the company will prepare your check from which some taxes will be withheld. The entire amount of the withdrawal becomes immediately taxable for federal and (if applicable) state and city income taxes. In addition to the normal income taxes, the federal government assesses a 10 percent penalty tax on the amount withdrawn. Some states and local taxing authorities also apply a penalty tax.

Thus, somewhere between 30 and 50 percent of the amount of money you withdraw from your 401(k) plan may go to taxes. It is important to note that your company will withhold only 20 percent of the taxes due. When you file your income tax returns, you must pay the rest. It is not uncommon for people to withdraw funds and spend all the proceeds. When April 15 arrives, they face a large tax bill for the additional taxes and penalty owed to the government—and no money to pay it. You may want to ask your company to withhold more than 20 percent from the withdrawal so the taxes are covered.

Remember, on a $10,000 withdrawal you may net only $5,000 to $7,000. You must set aside some of the funds to pay the taxes that will be due on your next income tax return.

It is a good idea to check with a tax advisor before making a 401(k) plan withdrawal to make sure that you have properly accounted for all the taxes.

In addition to all these taxes and penalties, some plans may prohibit you from saving in the plan for one year after you make an in-service withdrawal. During this time, you will lose the ability to build savings tax-free for your retirement.

Saving After Taxes for Early Withdrawal

Some 401(k) plans allow you to save money on an after-tax basis. After-tax savings do not give you the benefit of tax deferrals on the amount you contribute to the plan, but the investment earnings are not taxed until you make a withdrawal. Because you did not get a tax benefit for your contribution, it is much easier to withdraw these after-tax funds when you need them. Usually, your company requires less paperwork to make a withdrawal from the after-tax portion of your 401(k) account.

The contribution portion of your savings will not be taxed again when you ask for a withdrawal, but all of your investment earnings will be taxed and subject to early withdrawal penalties. Also, depending on the accounting system the company set up for your plan, you may have to withdraw a mix of pretax and after-tax savings.

If you think you are going to need some of your savings before retirement, make after-tax contributions to your plan. You will get all the other benefits of the 401(k) plan, including tax-free compounding, while your savings are in the plan.

When Should I Save After-Tax?

As a rule of thumb, you will be better off saving money outside the 401(k) plan or in the after-tax portion of the plan if you think you will need the funds during the next five years. For example, assume that you are saving to purchase a new home and can get the same investment returns outside the plan that you would have received in it. You can save more by paying the taxes on your earnings and investing in the after-tax portion of the 401(k) plan, mutual funds, bank or credit union savings account.

There is an exception, however. When your company matches a portion of your contribution to the 401(k) plan and you become fully vested (i.e., the company's matching contribution belongs to you if you withdraw from the plan), then you can save more on a pretax basis even with the 10 percent penalty tax. In this case, making a withdrawal to purchase a house or tuition makes financial sense. With the company's contribution, you will have more funds after paying all the taxes and the early withdrawal penalty than if you saved on your own in the after-tax part of the 401(k) plan or outside the plan.

Consequences of an In-Service Withdrawal

Even though it may make immediate financial sense to take a hardship withdrawal, you are doing serious damage to your long-run retirement savings goals. The amount of the withdrawal

---

Vesting

Once you start participating in the 401(k) plan, all of your contributions belong to you. What if your company matches a portion of your contribution?

The company's contributions become yours to take with you when you become vested in the plan. Vesting means that you have full rights to the company's contribution in the 401(k) plan.

In some plans, you become vested in a progressively greater percentage of the company's contribution in each passing year. In other plans, you become fully vested after a set number of years. The IRS requires that you become fully vested within five to seven years of joining the plan, although many companies will allow you to become fully invested within fewer years. Your company can provide you with a vesting schedule.

Under special circumstances—death, disability, or retirement—you become fully vested immediately.

---

reduces savings that will compound until retirement. Also, because you may be kept out of the plan for at least one year, you will have lost the ability to save tax free during that time period.

If you are over 40 years old, you will want to carefully consider taking a hardship withdrawal. An individual who starts in the plan at age 22, saves for 10 years, and then makes a withdrawal to purchase a home, still has time to recover from the decline in the savings balance more readily than someone who is much closer to retirement.

The Withdrawal Loophole

Older participants in a 401(k) plan may wish to consider another way to make an in-service withdrawal. If you are under age 59 1/2 (or age 55 and taking early retirement), you are allowed to make an annual withdrawal based on your life expectancy. Under these circumstances, you or your tax advisor needs to look at an actuarial table that determines life expectancy. For example, if the table lists your life expectancy as 30 years, you are allowed to withdraw

1/30th of your account balance. Each year you must make a similar withdrawal based on the actuarial table. Withdrawals made in
this manner will not be subject to the early withdrawal penalty,
but you still must pay ordinary income taxes on the amount you
withdraw. The rules that govern this type of withdrawal are complicated and not all plans are set up to allow for this kind of multi-
year distribution. Consult your company's benefits representative
and tax advisor if this method of withdrawing funds is appealing.

THE OTHER WAY TO MAKE A WITHDRAWAL: LOANS

The IRS did provide a way for you to get some of your money
temporarily before retirement: Take out a loan.

Companies have a great deal of flexibility in how they set up
their 401(k) plan loan programs. This book will cover only a few
of the general provisions typically found in loan programs. Your
benefits administrator can tell you if loans are offered and how
they are administered.

Many plans allow participants to borrow up to 50 percent of
their vested account balance (up to a maximum of $50,000). Unless
the loan is required for the purchase of a residence, the IRS requires
that you pay back the loan within five years. Loans for the purchase of residences may be extended over a longer time period.

Like a loan from a bank or credit union, you have to sign a
promissory note and the plan provides you with an amortization
schedule. You also have to pay interest on the amount you borrow.
The company is required to charge an interest rate that commer-
cial lenders would charge for a similar loan with similar collateral.
However, there is a lot less paperwork to fill out. Usually the loan
is paid back through automatic payroll deductions.

The best part is that the interest you pay on the loan is paid to
your individual account. Unlike borrowing from the bank where
you pay the bank the interest, you are borrowing the money from
yourself and paying yourself for the privilege. On the other hand,
when interest rates are low, you will be paying yourself a low return. During periods of low interest rates, other investments may
do much better and you will miss out on these higher returns
while you pay your loan back.

One asset allocation strategy that you may wish to use during the period of your loan is to increase your exposure to equity. Since the loan and the interest paid behaves like the safety of principal option, you could reduce your exposure in the investment options that have fixed-income characteristics.

If you default on the loan, the plan must notify the IRS and you will be taxed on the amount of the loan plus the 10 percent early withdrawal penalty, if applicable. When you leave the company before retirement, the loan becomes due immediately and must be paid back or it will be taxed as a distribution with the 10 percent penalty for participants under the age of 59 1/2.

401(k) plan loans are costly for the company to set up and administer. You can expect to pay an origination fee of at least $50 to $100, and additional expenses may be charged to your account.

WHAT HAPPENS WHEN I LEAVE THE COMPANY?

The savings in your 401(k) plan account belong to you. If you have vested in the account, your total savings will include your contributions, the company's contributions, and all the investment returns that have accrued to the account. If you have not been with the company long enough to be vested, you will not receive the company's contribution and the investment returns related to those contributions.

Included in the paperwork that you will be asked to fill out when you leave the company is a form from your 401(k) plan administrator. The form offers you several choices on what to do with your 401(k) plan savings balance. Let's review the possible choices.

Choice 1: Do Nothing

Until you reach your company's normal retirement age (65 years old for many organizations), your company cannot force you to take a withdrawal from the plan if the balance in your account is greater than $3,500. You may leave your 401(k) balance within the plan until you start making withdrawals for retirement. You will receive the same account statements and information as current employees. If you have a loan outstanding, the company may allow you to set up a monthly or quarterly repayment schedule and not require you to immediately pay off the loan.

Some companies may strongly encourage you to withdraw or roll over your account balance to an IRA or your new company's 401(k) plan. It is expensive for the company to hire administrative staff to maintain records for employees who no longer work for the organization. If the company encourages you to take a distribution, you should probably consider doing so. It is a signal that you will probably get only the minimum amount of information about your investment.

Choice 2: Ask for a Distribution

You may request the company to prepare a check for all your funds. This will be considered the same as an in-service withdrawal for which the company is required to withhold 20 percent for the payment of income taxes. The IRS will expect you to pay taxes on the rest of the distribution, plus the 10 percent penalty tax, when taxes are due the following year.

Like the in-service withdrawal, you will ultimately net only 50 or 60 percent of your funds after all the taxes are paid. You will also be reducing your retirement savings by a considerable amount. No financial planner would recommend this option unless you had a very serious and immediate need for cash, but the choice is yours to make.

Choice 3: IRA Rollover

You may request the company to roll over the account to an individual retirement account (IRA). This choice requires some advance planning. You must decide on an institution where you would like to open an IRA.

If your company uses one or two mutual fund companies for its investment choices, you may be able to roll over your account into the same funds that your company uses for the 401(k) plan. However, you can choose any institution that provides IRAs, including most banks, credit unions, stock brokerages, and all mutual fund companies that serve retail investors. Like the 401(k) plan, the IRA rollover leaves you in control of your assets and lets you make investment choices.

The rollover into an IRA account is *not* a taxable transaction. Taxes are deferred on the contributions and investment returns in the account until you begin making withdrawals. Again, like the 401(k) plan, if your make withdrawals before age 59 1/2, you will be faced with the 10 percent penalty tax in addition to income taxes at the usual rates.

Do not add your 401(k) investments into existing IRAs, especially those where you contributed after-tax savings. Establish new IRAs for your 401(k) rollovers. When you start making withdrawals after age 59 1/2, it will be much easier to account for the taxes you owe on the pretax and after-tax savings.

Furthermore, if you change your mind and decide to place the money from your 401(k) plan into your new employer's 401(k) plan, you can withdraw the money from an IRA that was set up especially to receive your 401(k) distribution. You won't have this option if you mix funds from your 401(k) plan with an existing IRA.

Tax regulations allow you to roll over your tax-deferred account to your IRA within 60 days of the distribution. Prior to January 1, 1993, your company could write you a check for the entire distribution of your 401(k) plan and, as long as you deposited the amount within 60 days into the IRA, there were no taxes on the distribution. Starting in 1993, your company is required to withhold 20 percent of any distribution for taxes. You must still roll over the remaining 80 percent within 60 days to the IRA, but you will not get your 20 percent back until you receive your tax refund the following year. If you want to contribute the full amount of the distribution to your IRA, you will have to come up with the additional 20 percent that was withheld from your own pocket.

You can avoid the 20 percent withholding if you direct your company to make the transfer directly into an IRA, or ask for the distribution check to be made out to you *and* the IRA institution. This ensures that your full 401(k) balance will be transferred tax free.

Choice 4: Rollover to Another 401(k) Plan

The company you are joining may allow a new employee to roll over assets from a previous employer's 401(k) plan into its 401(k) plan, if one is offered. (Not all companies allow you to do this, so check with your benefits representative.) Again, this type of rollover is completely tax free as long as your former employer sends the money directly to the new company's plan or prepares the check with your name and the name of the 401(k) plan. If the company provides you alone with the check, it is required by law to withhold 20 percent of the distribution.

Choice 5: Distribution Based on Life Expectancy

As you have read, if you choose to take equal annual payments based on your life expectancy, you can avoid paying any penalty taxes on your 401(k) plan distribution. Your tax advisor can calculate how much you can withdraw in each year. Older employees taking early retirement find this a very attractive option. You will be withdrawing only a small portion of your savings, so the balance continues to grow based on the returns of the investment options you have chosen.

For example, a 50-year-old employee who is single and leaves the company with a 401(k) account balance of $1,000,000 could expect to withdraw about $90,000 a year in equal annual installments based on the IRS mortality tables. Each year participants can recalculate the amount to withdraw based on their current age and life expectancy, so the amount of the withdrawal can change each year. Recalculating the amount to withdraw can be advantageous, particularly after several years of large investment gains allow you to increase the amount you withdraw.

IRA versus 401(k) Plan

Assuming you want to preserve your retirement savings, which is better: to roll over your savings into an IRA or into your new employer's 401(k) plan?

There is no clear-cut answer to this question. The advantage of the IRA is that you have complete control of the investment options. You can establish an IRA at one of the large mutual fund families like Fidelity, Vanguard, or American Funds or the thousands of other institutions that offer IRAs. This enables you to invest in dozens of different funds. You can move your funds back and forth as you see fit.

The IRA offers investment options that may not be available in your new company's 401(k) plan. For example, if your new employer does not offer an international fund, you could use your IRA to make that investment, while you invest in U.S. equity and fixed-income funds through your new company's 401(k) plan.

On the other hand, you cannot borrow money from an IRA, so if your new company's 401(k) plan offers loans to participants—and you are otherwise satisfied with its investment options—the savings will help you qualify for larger loan amounts immediately upon employment.

Another reason to use your new company's 401(k) plan is to take advantage of five year forward income tax averaging of lump sum distributions. This distribution technique provides considerable tax savings benefits for some individuals (see Chapter 8). It is available only when you take a lump sum distribution from a 401(k) plan or other company-sponsored tax-qualified retirement plans and is not available to distributions from an IRA.

Finally, you may feel more comfortable with all your savings in one plan. This certainly requires less effort on your part to keep track of all your savings balances.

Whether you elect to take a distribution of the funds or roll them over into a new IRA or 401(k) plan, keep all the documentation that your company sends you. These papers are essential to determining your tax basis when you start making withdrawals.

What to Do with Company Stock

If one of your 401(k) investments is company stock, so far all of the distributions discussed assume that you will sell the company stock back to the plan and take a cash distribution. But you may believe your company's stock price is likely to appreciate in value, so you need to consider the pros and cons of taking your distribution in shares instead of cash.

The advantage of taking stock is that you continue to defer any capital gains that you have earned on the stock. It's your option; you can either recognize the capital gains and pay the taxes on the increased value of the stock, or you can continue to defer the taxes by rolling over the shares into an IRA. When you roll over the stock into an IRA, you will not have to pay any tax on the dividends earned and price appreciation until you sell the stock and withdraw the proceeds from the IRA.

Suppose the average price of all your stock purchases is $30 per share and the stock is now selling for $40 per share. You can take the stock certificates and avoid paying taxes on the $10 of capital gains. Like other withdrawals that have been discussed, your withdrawal of company stock is still subject to taxes and penalties if the shares are not rolled over directly into an IRA.

In this example, taxes and penalties would apply to the $30 average share price. The extra $10 per share would not be taxed until the shares are sold. Thus, if you want to hold the stock outside of an IRA, you could avoid some of the taxes until you sell the stock.

If the shares are held in the IRA and you sold the stock for $40 per share, the taxing of the $10 per share capital gains on the sale of the stock would not take place until you take a distribution from the account. Not all IRA trustees will accept stock. Before asking your company to transfer stock, find an IRA trustee that will accept corporate securities. Most major stock brokerage firms will accept stock, but many banks and mutual fund IRAs will not. If you would like a brokerage firm to hold the stock certificates, but use a mutual fund company for the rest of your savings, it may be possible for your company to distribute the company stock certificates to one IRA trustee and the remaining assets to another IRA trustee or 401(k) plan. You will have to ask for this kind of distribution, because it is not likely to be one of the choices offered to you.

OTHER TYPES OF DISTRIBUTIONS BEFORE RETIREMENT

Several other circumstances may require a distribution from a 401(k) plan before retirement.

Qualified Domestic Relations Order (QDRO)

If you divorce your spouse and the court divides your 401(k) assets between the two of you, it will issue a Qualified Domestic Relations Order (QDRO). In this circumstance, your company can distribute assets to your ex-spouse, and the IRS will not charge the 10 percent penalty tax. However, the proceeds from the distribution will be taxed at ordinary income tax rates unless the funds are rolled over into an IRA.

Disability

A totally disabled employee who can no longer work is allowed to take a distribution from the 401(k) plan without the penalty tax. The distribution will be taxed at ordinary income tax rates unless the funds are invested in an IRA.

Death

When you signed up for the 401(k) plan, you were required to fill out a form in which you named a beneficiary. (If you skipped that line, your estate becomes the beneficiary.) If you die and you named your spouse as the beneficiary, your assets can be distributed without the penalty tax. He or she will have the same options that you had upon leaving the company. The survivor can either roll over the distribution into an IRA or pay income taxes on it.

A person other than a spouse who is named as the beneficiary will have to pay ordinary income taxes on the distribution. However, under these circumstances the tax code exempts the first $5,000 from taxes. In the case of a distribution due to death or disability, your 401(k) account becomes fully vested, if it wasn't already, so your company's contribution will be part of the distribution.

SUMMARY

- The 401(k) plan is somewhat more complicated than a bank or credit union savings account. There are limits to the amount you can invest. Your company may have to apply additional limits for the plan to satisfy the IRS rules on nondiscrimination testing.
- Early withdrawals from the plan are limited. Only in financial hardship can the company allow you to withdraw your funds.
- When you withdraw funds from a 401(k) plan before age 59½, you not only have to pay income tax at your regular rates but also pay the IRS an additional 10 percent penalty tax. If you live in a high-tax state, you will net only about one-half of the amount you withdraw.
- 401(k) plans are portable. When you leave your company, you can roll over your 401(k) plan account balance to your new employer's 401(k) plan or into an IRA. Rollovers avoid any taxes on the account balances.
- Rolling over company stock is more tricky, but it can be done if you set up an IRA with a brokerage firm.

Chapter Eight

Pension, 401(k), and Social Security: Putting It All Together for Retirement

T he whole purpose of the 401(k) plan is to enable you to save for retirement. While distributions prior to retirement age—59 1/2 under IRS regulations—are allowed, they are strongly discouraged with the use of a 10 percent penalty tax. By setting up the 401(k) plan, your company is encouraging you to save for your retirement.

Saving is one thing, but you must also plan for your retirement. When you reach retirement, you will be required to make many decisions about your savings and other benefits provided by your employer. You will have to live with the consequences of these decisions throughout your retirement. For most people retiring at age 65, that means at least 20 years.

Imagine, decisions you make today will have to satisfy all your needs for the next 20 years! When you are faced with major decisions like these, it is only natural to want to learn all the ramifications of the alternatives from which you must choose and plan accordingly. Knowing the types of decisions you will have to make when you retire is essential. It is never too early to start thinking about retirement strategies.

NATE AND REBECCA

Nate and Rebecca have worked in corporate jobs throughout their careers. Nate, who is now 64, plans to retire next year. Rebecca, who is 60, is thinking about taking early retirement at the same time. They were married in their late 20s and have saved a little over $1.5 million in their 401(k) and IRA plans. Although they work for different companies, both companies will provide Nate and Rebecca with a pension benefit, and both will be eligible for Social Security.

It is no accident that Nate and Rebecca accumulated such a large savings balance in their 401(k) plans. Rebecca, who always managed the family's finances, began thinking about retirement shortly after they were married. Even while raising two children and saving for their college education, Rebecca put the maximum amount allowed into her 401(k) plan and encouraged Nate to do the same. The family made some sacrifices, but they were not very painful, thanks to the automatic payroll deductions for their 401(k) plans. Rebecca changed companies three times during her career and Nate changed jobs four times. In each case, they rolled over their savings into IRA plans. When making asset allocation decisions in their 401(k) plans, they considered the investments in their IRAs.

Throughout her career, Rebecca's portfolio was heavily weighted in equity and growth equity options, while she encouraged Nate to be more conservative and to use the balanced fund and income fund offered by his company's plan. Together their portfolios averaged about 70 percent equity and 30 percent fixed income. In the last five years, she changed their joint asset allocation to 50 percent equity, increasing the amount of fixed income.

In her early 40s, Rebecca learned about replacement ratios and developed a strategy for retirement. She determined that their goal should be a 90 percent replacement ratio, because she and Nate planned to travel extensively when they reached retirement. Every five years, she checked with the Social Security Administration to make sure that their accounts were properly credited with the years of service.

In their mid-50s, Rebecca and Nate set up appointments with benefit representatives at their respective companies to learn how each company handled retirement payments. They were interested in lump sum distributions, annuity payments, and an estimated calculation of benefits they would receive at age 60, 62, and 65. In short, they wanted to know if early retirement was feasible for them.

Based on the information learned at these meetings, they decided it would be best if Nate worked until 65. His company didn't provide postretirement medical benefits, so Nate would need to wait until age 65 when he was eligible for Medicare. Rebecca, on the other hand, thought that she might be able to retire early because her company did offer postretirement medical benefits that would help her with any medical problems until she was 65.

As they approached retirement, they read several books on personal finance, subscribed to a personal finance magazine, and attended seminars at their companies. They developed a budget for the first five years of their retirement.

As a result of their planning, Rebecca and Nate retired with a plan that minimized taxes and gave them confidence that they would not outlive their retirement savings.

RETIREMENT REQUIRES PLANNING

There is no question that retirement represents a major change in lifestyle for anyone working in a corporation. People who work for corporations throughout their careers receive a paycheck every week, two weeks, or month. More than likely, medical insurance covers catastrophic and major medical expenses.

Upon retirement, you have to see that you are "paid" an appropriate salary. You need to determine how much to pay yourself so that your savings last for the rest of your life. You have to have medical insurance. The government helps with some of this expense through Medicare, but most retirees also purchase Medigap insurance—a supplementary form of medical insurance that pays many of the medical expenses not covered by Medicare. You need to be especially careful that you have budgeted for high-ticket expenses such as buying an automobile. How do you learn about all this? How should you go about making these decisions?

There are numerous sources of information. This book covers most of the main topics. See References for materials that specialize in retirement planning. Talk to your company benefits representative about planning for retirement. Find out if your company offers seminars for employees nearing retirement. Finally, you may want to consult with a financial planner or tax advisor for investment advice now and during retirement.

YOUR REPLACEMENT RATIO

The replacement ratio is a good place to start in the development of your retirement plan. Suppose you are nearing retirement and are earning $50,000 per year. You have a satisfactory lifestyle that you would like to maintain when you retire. How much money will you need each year?

Assuming that your children have grown and that expenses are for you and your spouse only, chances are you will need less than $50,000 a year. After all, you will no longer have the expense of commuting and buying work clothes, and perhaps your meal expenses will be reduced. Your home mortgage may be paid off. Your income tax bill will probably drop because you will no longer be earning a salary and you are in a lower tax bracket. In addition, you may not need to save as much money.

The replacement ratio is the percentage comparison between preretirement and postretirement income. A common rule of thumb among financial planners is people need a 70 to 80 percent replacement ratio to maintain the same standard of living from preretirement to postretirement. In other words, if you are living on a salary of $50,000 a year before retirement, you will need $35,000 to $40,000 to live on in retirement.

Don't forget inflation. Just as your salary grows with inflation and promotions, so do you have to cope with inflation after you retire. If $40,000 a year is enough in your first year of retirement, you will probably need about $60,000 a year in your 10th year of retirement to keep the same standard of living, assuming inflation grows at 4 percent per year.

You may need a higher replacement ratio than 70 to 80 percent, for needs beyond inflation. If you plan to travel extensively, purchase a new retirement home, start a small business, or have other financial needs, you may need a higher replacement ratio. This is especially true in the early years of retirement.

SOURCES OF RETIREMENT INCOME

After you have determined the correct replacement ratio for your lifestyle, you must figure out how to achieve it. More than likely, you will have at least two sources of income when you retire.

Social Security

First, you have Social Security. The size of this benefit will depend on how long you have contributed to Social Security and your age at retirement. To find out how much you will receive from Social Security, you can call your local Social Security office or call 800–772–1213 and request Form SSA-7004. When you have filled out this form and returned it to Social Security, you will receive a report that shows how much you have contributed throughout your career and an estimate of how much your benefit will be upon retirement. It is a good practice to get this report at least every five years to make sure that the Social Security Administration is properly crediting your account. According to current law, the Social Security Administration is not required to fix errors it made more than five years ago. You don't want to apply for your benefits, only to discover that the Social Security Administration has been crediting someone else's account because a clerk entered the wrong Social Security number 20 years ago!

Pension Benefits

Next, your company may offer a pension plan. Depending on your company's pension plan design, you may be allowed to take a lump sum distribution or convert your benefit to an annuity. If your company doesn't offer the lump sum alternative, you will be required to take a fixed monthly payment for the rest of your life. Usually, you can either elect to receive a fixed payment for your life or choose the joint and survivor option. The latter pays a smaller monthly payment, but your spouse continues to receive a monthly payment after your death until he or she dies. The law requires you to obtain your spouse's consent to establish any form of annuity other than the joint and survivor option. The amount of these payments is based on your salary, years of service, and age at retirement.

401(k) Plan and IRA Distributions

As long as you have retired after age 55, you can begin taking distributions from your IRA and 401(k) plans without any penalty taxes. For the exception to this rule, see the explanation of distributions based on life expectancy in Chapter 7. You pay income tax on the distributions, just as you pay taxes on your pension benefits and a portion of your Social Security payments.

Other Sources of Income

You may have other sources of income from self-employment, interest on savings accounts, dividends, rental real estate, life insurance policies, trusts, and so on. All should be considered when reviewing your sources of retirement income.

VISITING YOUR BENEFITS REPRESENTATIVE

To estimate your replacement ratio, you need more information than can be provided in a book. First, look at your company's annual benefits statement. Some companies provide their employees with a comprehensive statement that shows how much retirement income they might expect to receive at various ages of early retirement and at age 65.

If you don't receive an annual statement or would like an explanation of your current statement, make an appointment with your benefits representative. Tell the representative that you are doing preretirement planning and would like some help estimating the amount of your retirement benefits. Many companies have computer programs that allow you to enter your age, salary, 401(k) assets, estimated growth rates, and other data about your personal financial situation. These programs can show you several retirement scenarios and how much you can expect to receive from Social Security, pension, and the 401(k) plan.

Potential Sources of Retirement Income

Wages
Income from self-employment
Pension
Social Security
Investment income from lump sum retirement plan payout
Interest from savings and bond investments
Dividends from stock investments
Distributions from IRAs and 401(k) plans
Distributions from employee stock ownership plans (ESOPs)
Income from rental real estate
Income from trusts
Other

Questions to Ask Your Benefits Representative

1. Does the company have a pension plan?
2. Based on my current salary adjusted for inflation, what will be my monthly pension benefit at retirement? Provide the representative with the possible ages that you might like to retire. If the plan offers joint-survivor benefits, what would the payments be?
3. Can the pension benefit be taken as a lump sum payment?
4. Are there other retirement income benefits, such as an ESOP?
5. Does the company provide postretirement medical insurance? What does it cost?
6. When I retire, can I keep my funds in the 401(k) plan and make monthly or quarterly withdrawals? Or do I have to take an immediate lump sum distribution?
7. How long does it take to process all the retirement paperwork? When will I begin receiving payments from these various accounts?

WHAT SHOULD I DO WITH MY 401(k) SAVINGS?

When you retire, you must decide how to take your 401(k) plan benefit. The choices are similar to those discussed in Chapter 7, except the tax consequences are different and usually more favorable.

Choice 1: Do Nothing—Leave It in the 401(k) Plan

Some companies allow you to leave your 401(k) balance within the plan and make withdrawals as you need them. You receive account statements and information just as current employees do. If you have a loan outstanding, the company may even allow you to set up a monthly or quarterly repayment schedule and not require you to pay off the loan immediately.

Funds that you withdraw are taxed as ordinary income. If you make a partial withdrawal, you lose the ability to take a lump sum distribution (see choice 3).

If you are comfortable with the investment options provided by your 401(k) plan and are pleased with the level of service, leaving your 401(k) balance in the plan is an ideal option. Chances are that fees are equal to or less than those charged by a mutual fund company, bank, or insurance company where you might roll over your assets to maintain an IRA. On the other hand, the service may be slower. Ask how long it takes to receive distributions from the plan. Ask whether an automatic monthly or quarterly replacement ratio can be set up so that you can receive checks on a regular basis.

Choice 2: Installment Payments or Annuity

Some companies will agree to distribute your 401(k) plan savings in installments. For example, the company might agree to pay you $500 per month from the 401(k) plan until your account is exhausted or until you die. If you die, your heirs will receive the account balance. Under the installment method, your funds will continue to be invested as you direct and will continue to accumulate tax free. If you choose this method of distribution, you forgo any possibility of taking the funds in a lump sum and taking advantage of the favorable tax treatment described under choice 3.

Similarly, some companies will allow you to convert your savings to an annuity. The annuity is nearly identical to the monthly benefit payments that your company pays under the pension plan. Indeed, some companies will combine the payments from your pension plan with an annuity payout from your 401(k) plan.

With an annuity, you become a beneficiary and are paid a fixed amount of money each month until you die. If you choose a joint survivor payment, your spouse (a second beneficiary) continues to receive the payments until he or she dies. In either case, the monthly payment never changes and a check is received each month. Unfortunately, the monthly payment of fixed-income annuities does not grow with inflation. Twenty years of inflation might make your fixed-income payment look pretty small. Some participants dislike the annuity option because no money from this source goes into their estate upon the death of the beneficiaries.

Choice 3: The Lump Sum Distribution

You may request the company to prepare a check for all your funds. This is called a lump sum distribution. The lump sum distribution may receive favorable tax treatment if it meets the following conditions:

1. The lump sum distribution is made within one tax year. You cannot take part of the distribution in one year and the remainder in another year.

2. The lump sum distribution represents all of your savings in the plan. You are taking all your funds and "closing" your account.

3. All of your company's retirement plans that are the same type as a 401(k) have to be considered one plan. If your company has other defined contribution plans, such as a profit-sharing plan or employee stock ownership plan (ESOP), you must take lump sum distributions from these plans in the same year you take your 401(k) plan distribution. The typical defined benefit pension plan is not considered the same type of plan as a 401(k) plan.

4. You have participated in the plan for five or more years and are over 59 1/2 years old.

TABLE 8–1
Examples of Five Year Forward Averaging

Lump Sum Distribution	Federal Taxes Due	Taxes as a Percent of Distribution
$ 20,000	$ 1,500	7.5
50,000	6,900	13.8
100,000	15,000	15.0
200,000	42,058	21.0
500,000	133,273	26.7

If you had to pay normal income tax rates on these lump sum distributions, the taxes as a percent of the distribution would probably be greater than 30%.

Five year forward income tax averaging. When the lump sum distribution meets these tests, you can apply five year forward income averaging on the entire distribution. This favorable tax treatment is now available only once in your lifetime. (Five- and 10-year averaging used on distributions prior to 1987 do not apply to this once-in-a-lifetime limit.) If you were 50 years old in 1986, you also may be eligible for 10 year forward income averaging treatment.

Forward income averaging is a technique that calculates the taxes owed as if they were distributed equally over five years. This technique significantly reduces the amount of income taxes paid. You should consult an accountant or tax advisor before electing to receive your benefits in a lump sum distribution.

When you take the lump sum alternative, you either pay ordinary income taxes or receive the one-time benefit of forward income averaging on the balance. The result is that you have paid all the necessary income taxes on your savings. In effect, you have paid back the government's tax-deferred loan that you accumulated while saving for retirement.

If you invest the funds after paying these taxes, you have only to pay taxes on interest or dividend income and realized capital gains. While this may seem like a good idea, remember that you have substantially reduced your savings, perhaps by as much as 40 percent, to pay all these taxes. If you don't have an immediate need for the funds, you should consider rolling over the lump sum distribution into an IRA.

The success penalty. There is one other caveat with a lump sum distribution. If the lump sum distribution from all your plans exceeds $750,000, the IRS applies a so-called success penalty of an extra 15 percent tax on the amount above $750,000. For example, on a $1,000,000 distribution from a 401(k) plan, you pay the usual taxes (ordinary income taxes or the five year forward averaging taxes) on the first $750,000. On the remaining $250,000, you pay the ordinary income taxes *plus* 15 percent of $250,000, or $37,500. Consult a tax advisor if this situation applies to you. Strategies using annuities and other investments can help minimize the penalty tax.

Choice 4: IRA Rollover

When you qualify for a lump sum distribution, you may request the company to roll over the account to an individual retirement account (IRA). The procedure is the same as rolling over your account to an IRA when you switch jobs. You must select an institution and ask your company to send the funds directly to the institution that will act as trustee for the IRA in order to avoid withholding taxes. (See Chapter 7 on how to roll over your distribution into an IRA.)

WHICH CHOICE IS RIGHT FOR YOU?

No one can select the correct strategy for your retirement needs. You must judge how comfortable you are with managing your own affairs or having someone else make the decisions for you. That's essentially the choice between the annuity option and all the others.

The Annuity Strategy

When you select an annuity, you have chosen to receive a fixed payment each month for the rest of your life and, if you picked the joint survivor option, the life of your spouse. Assuming that you have an annuity payment from your pension plan and are receiving Social Security benefits, the bulk of your retirement income is in the form of fixed monthly payments.

The problem is inflation. Of your three sources of annuities—401(k), pension, and Social Security—only the Social Security benefits are adjusted regularly for inflation. To make up for the long-term effects of inflation, you should continue a regular savings program after retirement.

What? You have retired and you have to continue to save? The answer is yes! For at least the first 10 years of retirement, you should save 5 to 10 percent of your income.

As you read in Chapters 3 and 5, you should set up an asset allocation to help you beat inflation. An allocation of 40 to 50 percent equity at age 65 is not unreasonable. At age 75, you may still want to have 10 to 20 percent of your savings in equity funds.

The annuity payments from your retirement plans and Social Security benefits provide both stable monthly payments and the ability to withstand the volatility of the equity markets. Later in retirement, as inflation reduces the value of the fixed monthly payments, your savings should be large enough so that you can withdraw funds each month to maintain your standard of living.

The Installment or IRA Strategy

Whether you choose to leave your savings in the 401(k) plan and take installment payments or roll over your funds into an IRA, you have chosen to make your own investment decisions. Unlike the annuity, there is no guarantee that your savings will last until you die. You are responsible for ensuring that your savings last throughout your retirement years.

In this choice, you receive fixed monthly payments from Social Security and perhaps a company pension plan. Your savings continue to be invested in a tax-deferred savings vehicle.

The key to this strategy is developing and sticking to a budget. Each year, you should develop a detailed budget that includes not only normal monthly expenses but also any one-time expenses such as the purchase of a new car, a vacation trip, or home repairs or remodeling. This budget enables you to determine how much to withdraw from your IRA or 401(k) plan.

Next, take this budget and extend it for four more years. Add 4 to 5 percent per year to your normal monthly expenditures to cover rising inflation. Anticipate any large one-time expenses that you might face. The budget will give you a clear picture of your five-year expenditures.

On the income side, multiply your monthly payments from Social Security and other regular fixed-income sources by 12 to obtain the first year's income. Then multiply the first year's result by 5 to obtain the 5-year-income figure. Subtract income from expenditures. The result is the expected amount of savings withdrawals that will be required over the next five years.

You should invest this required five-year sum in safety of principal options. That means investing your funds in money market mutual funds, CDs, or short-term bond funds.

Because the remaining funds will be needed after five years, you should develop an asset allocation that will provide sufficient growth to beat inflation. An asset allocation of 40 to 50 percent in equity funds early in retirement and 10 to 20 percent in equity funds later in retirement is not unreasonable.

Does all this planning sound like too much work? If so, the annuity strategy may be better for you. Or you might consider paying a financial planning consultant to help you structure your retirement investment portfolio and develop the necessary budgets (see Appendix).

How Long Will Your Money Last?

Before you start drawing on investments in retirement, you should do some advance planning to ensure that the money will last as long as you do. Table 8–2 can help. For example, if the value of your retirement account grows at a rate of 8 percent a

TABLE 8–2
How Many Years Will Your Money Last?

		Rate of Withdrawal of Original Capital										
		6%	7%	8%	9%	10%	11%	12%	13%	14%	15%	16%
Rate of	12%	—	—	—	—	—	—	—	22	17	14	12
Account	11%	—	—	—	—	—	—	23	17	14	12	11
Growth	10%	—	—	—	—	—	25	18	15	13	11	10
	9%	—	—	—	—	26	20	16	14	12	11	10
	8%	—	—	—	28	20	16	14	12	11	9	9
	7%	—	—	30	22	17	14	12	11	10	9	8
	6%	—	33	23	18	15	13	11	10	9	8	8
	5%	36	25	20	16	14	12	11	9	9	8	7

Source: *The American Funds Investor,* published by the American Funds Group.

year and you are taking out 15 percent of your original capital each year, the money will last nine years. Cut your withdrawals to 10 percent and the money won't run out for 20 years.

You also can use Table 8–2 to gear your withdrawals to the length of time you want the money to last. Suppose you decide your savings must last 15 years and you estimate they will grow at an annual rate of 10 percent. In that case, you can withdraw roughly 13 percent of the value of your original capital each year. A dash in the space means that at that rate of withdrawal and expected return, your savings will never be exhausted.

WHEN YOU MUST TAKE DISTRIBUTIONS

Up to this point, the underlying assumption in developing your retirement strategy is that you have retired sometime after the age of 59 1/2, usually around the age of 65. But today more and more people are deferring the age of retirement beyond age 65. They are healthy and enjoy working.

However, when you reach age 70 1/2 another tax provision takes effect: The IRS requires that you begin taking distributions from your IRA or 401(k) plan. The minimum distributions are based on the total amount of your account and the use of actuarial tables that calculate your life expectancy. Should you choose to withdraw jointly with your spouse, both your and your spouse's age are considered in determining the amount of the distribution, resulting in a lower minimum distribution. IRS publication 575, *Pension and Annuity Income,* describes how to calculate the minimum withdrawal.

At age 70$1/2$, withdrawals are required even if you are still working. Each year, you could still be contributing to the 401(k) plan and taking a minimum withdrawal.

In addition, another success penalty is involved. The IRS calls it an *excess distribution penalty.* If your annual distribution exceeds $150,000, the amount of the distribution in excess of $150,000 is subject to a 15 percent penalty tax. The $150,000 floor for the excess distribution penalty is indexed to inflation and will be raised each year. If your total tax-deferred savings exceed $750,000, it is important to have a qualified tax advisor help you with these calculations. It might be necessary to take distributions from your IRA and 401(k) plans prior to age 70$1/2$ to avoid paying penalty taxes on the distributions.

SUMMARY

- It's never too early to begin planning for retirement. Learn the ground rules in your 40s and 50s. Later, develop a strategy for what to do with your retirement savings.
- Decide on an appropriate replacement ratio for the lifestyle you want to lead during retirement. Your personal replacement ratio will be a combination of pension benefits, Social Security benefits, 401(k) plan savings, and any other assets you own.
- Read your company's benefit statement and set up a meeting with your benefits representative. Call Social Security and obtain a form to check your account.
- About five years before retirement, learn about the ways you can have access to your funds. Decide whether you want to

take a lump sum distribution, roll over your account to an
IRA, or leave the assets in your company's plan.

- Develop an investment strategy for retirement. You need to
  have some of your assets in equity investments to beat long-
  term inflation.
- Keep five year's worth of income in short-term investment
  vehicles such as CDs, money market funds, and short-term
  bond funds. The asset allocation of the rest of your retirement
  savings should include equity investments.
- At age 70$\frac{1}{2}$, you must begin taking distributions and paying
  taxes on them. If your distributions exceed $150,000 a year,
  you pay a success penalty.

Appendix to Chapter Eight

TIPS ON CHOOSING A FINANCIAL PLANNER AND TAX ADVISOR

10 QUESTIONS YOU SHOULD ASK ON YOUR FIRST INTERVIEW

Any reputable financial planner should be willing to respond fully to the following 10 questions. If you don't like what you hear—or if the person refuses to cooperate—move on immediately. But even if the planner seems friendly and competent, double-check the responses wherever that's possible.

1. **Are you registered with the federal Securities and Exchange Commission and your state securities department?** Most financial planners are supposed to register with the SEC. In addition, all but seven states and the District of Columbia require that most planners register with the state's securities department. By itself, registering doesn't guarantee that a planner is honest or competent, but it does show that the planner knows the law and obeys it. Says Barbara Roper, Director of Investor Protection for the Consumer Federation of America in Washington, D.C.: "Registration is the absolute minimum to look for."

2. **What is your educational and professional backgound?** Unlike lawyers and accountants, planners typically are not legally required to have training or experience, so it is important to check credentials. Planners who have passed examinations in subjects such as investing, insurance, and estate planning can call themselves one of the following: certified financial planner, chartered financial consultant, chartered life underwriter, or personal financial specialist. At the very least, such designations indicate some knowledge of planning basics.

Ruth Simon, "Financial Planning's Broker Promise," *Money*, November 1992. Reprinted by special permission; copyright 1992, Time, Inc.

3. **What types of financial planning services do you provide?** Some planners specialize in one or two areas, such as retirement planning, insurance, or taxes. Make sure the planner you choose can address your particular concerns.

4. **Do you sell products or services other than providing investment advice to clients?** This question can alert you to potential conflicts of interest. Also check whether your planner sells only products sponsored by his or her company.

5. **What types of products do you recommend?** "You want to find out if a planner suggests good old-fashioned stuff like government securities, municipal bonds, common stocks, and mutual funds in addition to newfangled products such as limited partnerships, unit trusts, and insurance," says Mary Calhoun, a securities arbitration consultant.

6. **Will you disclose in advance your total compensation—including the commissions you will get for selling particular products, as well as your general fees?** The fact that a planner stands to earn commissions isn't necessarily a negative. But you should make sure that your needs—and not the commissions—determine which products you'll get pitched. For example, duck if your planner tries to fill your portfolio with limited partnerships, which can carry commissions of 8 percent or more.

7. **Have you been the subject of disciplinary actions by any federal or state agency or professional regulatory body, or been involved in arbitration proceedings with former clients?** Be sure to verify the planner's answer with your state securities department and the SEC.

8. **Will you provide me with a copy of your ADV?** Discount the fancy brochures. The document you need is Part II of your planner's ADV form, which he or she must file with the state and the SEC and show on request. The form includes information about a planner's experience, investment strategies, and potential conflicts of interest.

9. **Will you provide me with the names and phone numbers of three clients you've counseled for at least two years?** Call these clients and ask whether they are satisfied, what types of returns they have been getting, and whether they expect to stay with the planner in the future. Then, if you can, get more names from them to check with as well.

10. **May I see three examples of plans and follow-up reports you've drawn up for other investors?** The original plans will tell you whether advice was tailored to individual clients. Follow-ups will show how skillfully the planner made adjustments as events unfolded.

References

ORGANIZATIONS

American Association of Retired Persons (AARP)
Founded in 1958, with headquarters in Washington, DC, the American Association of Retired Persons (AARP) strives to improve all aspects of living for older persons. Anyone over 50 years of age, retired or not, is eligible for membership. Among its various publications, *Money Matters* helps you choose a tax preparer, lawyer, financial planner, and real estate broker; *A Single Person's Guide to Retirement Planning* provides guidance on investing, insurance, and other financial topics. Write to AARP—Fulfillment, 60 E Street NW, Washington, DC 20049.

The Institute of Financial Planners
Call or write for their free publication: *Selecting a Qualified Financial Planning Professional*. The Institute of Financial Planners, 7600 East Eastman Avenue, Suite 301, Denver, CO 80231; 800–282–7526.

Investment Company Institute
Call or write for their free publications: *An Investor's Guide to Reading the Mutual Fund Prospectus* and *What Is a Mutual Fund?* Investment Company Institute, 1600 M Street, NW, Suite 600, Washington, DC 20036; 202–293–7700.

Social Security Administration
To find our how much you will receive from Social Security when you retire, you can call your local Social Security office or call 800–772–1213 and request Form SSA-7004. Once you fill out this form and return it, you will receive a report that shows how much you can expect to receive at various retirement ages.

BOOKS

Bogle, John C. *Bogle on Mutual Funds*. Chicago: Irwin Professional Publishing, 1993.

Gaudio, Peter E., and Virginia S. Nicols. *Your Retirement Benefits*. New York: John Wiley & Sons, 1992.

Hirsch, Michael D. *The Mutual Fund Wealth Builder*. New York: Harper-Collins, 1991.

Krefetz, Gerald. *The Basics of Investing*. Chicago: Dearborn Financial Publishing, 1992.

Lynch, Peter. *One Up on Wall Street*. New York: Simon and Schuster, 1989.

Spitz, William T. *Get Rich Slowly: Building Your Financial Future Through Common Sense*. New York: Macmillan, 1992.

Stowers, James E. *Yes You Can . . . Achieve Financial Independence*. Kansas City: Deer Publishing, 1992.

Underwood, Don, and Paul B. Brown. *Grow Rich Slowly: The Merrill Lynch Guide to Retirement Planning*. New York: Viking Penguin, 1993.

Williamson, Gordon K. *Sooner Than You Think: Mapping a Course for a Comfortable Retirement*. Chicago: Irwin Professional Publishing, 1993.

PERIODICALS

Money published by Time Inc.

Smart Money published by Hearst Corporation and Dow Jones & Company.

Worth published by Capital Publishing Company.

Kiplinger's Personal Finance Magazine published by The Kiplinger Washington Editors, Inc.

(All are available on larger newsstands.)

Index

Thank you for choosing Irwin Professional Publishing for your business information needs. If you are part of a corporation, professional association, or government agency, consider our newest option: Irwin custom publishing. This service helps you create your own customized books, training manuals, and other materials from your organization's resources, select chapters of our books, or both.

Irwin Professional Publishing books are also excellent resources for training/educational programs, premiums, and incentives. For information on volume discounts or custom publishing services, call Irwin Professional Publishing at 1-800-634-3966.

Other books of interest from Irwin Professional Publishing . . .

THE HANDBOOK FOR NO-LOAD FUND INVESTORS
Fourteenth Edition
Sheldon Jacobs
"A gold mine."
—*The Wall Street Journal*
"Solid how-to advice even seasoned investors find useful."
—*Forbes*
"The type of reference investors can read once and get helpful advice and then read again as they become more familiar with mutual fund investing."
—*Barron's*
Provides a complete guide to mutual fund investing, from picking the right funds to avoiding common mistakes. Covering more than 1,700 funds, this reliable, easy-to-use reference details 10 years of performance data that highlights long-term winners.
(560 pages)
ISBN: 0-7863-0271-2

MORNINGSTAR MUTUAL FUND 500
An In-Depth Look at 500 Select Mutual Funds from the Leading Authority in Mutual-Fund Analysis, 1994 Edition
Morningstar, Inc.
An indispensable reference guide for any mutual fund investor, Morningstar Mutual Fund 500 provides a clear, unbiased review of 500 of the best-performing funds for 1994. Provides information on people running these elite funds, the securities that drive performance, and the yearly track record each fund has posted.
(300 pages)
ISBN: 0-7863-0136-8

HOW TO PICK THE BEST NO-LOAD MUTUAL FUNDS FOR SOLID GROWTH AND SAFETY
Sheldon Jacobs
Written by one of the most recognized names in the industry, this one-hour guide explains how to evaluate different types of funds. This is the ideal guide for individuals starting a long-range investment program for paying college expenses or planning retirement. (300 pages)
ISBN: 1-55623-574-7

BOGLE ON MUTUAL FUNDS
New Perspectives for the Intelligent Investor
John C. Bogle
A Fortune Book® Club Main Selection!
"Advice and philosophy with a provocative edge."
—The New York Times
More than 100,000 copies sold! Known as the "father of the index fund" and a "crusader of the industry," John C. Bogle is the nation's most experienced authority on mutual fund investing. In Bogle on Mutual Funds, he shares his wealth of wisdom and expertise, explaining not only the basic principles of mutual fund investing, but revealing the unique nuances and subtleties of this alluring field. (320 pages)
ISBN: 1-55623-860-6

Available at fine bookstores and libraries everywhere.